ARMCHAIR TYCOON

How to Make Money on the Stock Market
Without Knowing a Thing about Business

MALCOLM STACEY

Robson Books

First published in Great Britain in 1997 by Robson Books Ltd, Bolsover House, 5–6 Clipstone Street, London W1P 8LE

Copyright © 1997 Malcolm Stacey

The right of Malcolm Stacey to be identified as author of this work has been asserted by him in accordance with the Copyright Designs and Patents Act 1988

British Library Cataloguing in Publication Data
A catalogue record for this title is available from the British Library

ISBN 1 86105 124 7

Illustrations by JIM HUTCHINGS

All rights reserved. No part of this publication may be reproduced, stored in a retrieval system, or transmitted in any form or by any means, electronic, mechanical, photocopying, recording or otherwise, without the prior permission in writing of the publishers.

Photoset in North Wales by Derek Doyle & Associates, Mold, Flintshire. Printed in Great Britain by Creative Print & Design Wales, Ebbw Vale.

For Robin

Acknowledgements

Thanks to Jo Perkins, Eleri Jack, Alice Moulding, Douglas Waring, Richard Frederiks, Kathy Fletcher, Jody Daniels, Michala Richards, Leslie Watts, Arnold Wordsworth, Gillian Whitehouse, John Howard, Angie Knight, Debbie Higgins, David Berry, Richard Wachman, David Mitchell, Bhupinder Kholi, Paul Cummings, Cyril Mitchell, Margaret Collins, Ray Tiffany, Ian Dick, Nance Parry, Janet Spittal, James Watt, Trevor Barnes, Hazel Castell, Shirley Cummings, Peter Van Gelder, Edward Lythe, Carolyn Desourdy, Stewart Hilton, Nicky Thompson, Phil Peel, Selina Haniff, Oscar Rodriguez-Aguilar, Chris Diaz, Peter Burton, Stephen Smith, Bob Bilham, Liz Birkby, John Dymock, Evelyn Foster, Simon Dench, the Mitford Road Investment Club and ProShare (UK) Ltd.

Serious Wealth Warning

As investing on the stock exchange calls is a serious undertaking, please take time to read this:

Investments in shares can go down as well as up. You can make losses as well as gains, and may not recover the value of your investment. The publishers and the author accept no legal responsibilities for the contents of this book. Neither do they accept responsibility for any errors or omissions. The work is certainly not a substitute for qualified financial advice and you are strongly recommended to seek such professional advice before investing on the stock market. There are no suggestions that you should deal in shares in a specific company in this book. Any mention of a company is for illustrative purposes only and should not be taken as a recommendation to invest in it. Conditions in the money market are constantly changing – and may alter after publication of this work.

Contents

Preface

While working as an investigative reporter for BBC Radio Four, Malcolm Stacey has met and interviewed hundreds of people who are in daily contact with the City. They include heads of conglomerates, bankers, brokers, market analysts, chiefs of financial watchdogs, columnists, economists, civil servants, MPs and government ministers.

The purpose of these meetings with City experts was to shed light on a financial scandal or unfair practice affecting listeners. But later, in his spare time, Malcolm Stacey often rang up his contacts. After making it clear that he was now acting on his own private behalf, he asked two questions of them. The first was, 'Do you or any of your friends or colleagues trade in stocks and shares?' If the answer was 'Yes', he put his second question: 'Can you give any advice on how to make money from the stock market?'

Some of the experts could not help, but many did. And over five years, Malcolm wrote up all the answers in a special log which he called 'The Oracle'. The original idea was to provide a fund of advice to help himself, friends and relatives to have an 'edge' when punting on the stock market. Then, realising that more people are now turning to share investment in their hundreds of thousands, he decided to make a compilation of the best of his superb original collection of hints. *Armchair Tycoon* is the result.

None of the experts who supplied tips are mentioned by name in

Armchair Tycoon. This is for two reasons. Firstly, it was not known when the experts were asked for advice that a book was to be written, and therefore consent to name the contributors was not sought. Secondly, for hundreds of different reasons, not everyone likes it to be known that they buy and sell shares.

How to present the book was a problem. Malcolm Stacey could have simply published a long list of tips. Yet this would make pretty daunting reading. So he wrote *Armchair Tycoon* in the style a share guru might use to relate his own advice and experiences. A tiny few of the hints are Malcolm's own work, but the greatest part of the material is selected from hundreds of tips in 'The Oracle'.

There is no advice about any individual companies in *Armchair Tycoon* – it would soon be out of date. Nevertheless, this unique collection of 'rules of thumb' will prove invaluable for both beginners and experienced investors who want to improve performance by polishing their technique.

Malcolm is a dedicated share investor. He has gained a modest fortune since the Big Bang in 1986 starting from an original investment of £1,000. All the hints in this book have worked for him at some time or other. We hope they will help you, too. Sadly, like all other advice offered on share trading, heart-warming results can't be guaranteed. But then you know that already, don't you?

Introduction

I am grateful to this book for managing to tear me away from the telly. You see, most of my working day is spent watching share prices jumping about on teletext. I am hopelessly absorbed by this daily ritual. Like a gypsy with a tea-cup, I try to make sense of it all with a view to making money.

If I'm not watching the box, I bury my head in the *Financial Times*. But when I started to search for books on equity investments, I found only two kinds. Those which give you facts and figures about the workings of the Stock Exchange and those which examine the investment philosophy of just one individual, usually tremendously rich and known as a 'share guru'.

Some guru books are very good, but they tend to follow 'one grand design'. A common example of this master plan is to invest lots of money in a few well-established, highly respected blue-chip companies and leave it there for a long, long, long time. This strategy, which is also touched on in this book, has proved successful in the past. I recommend it to you. But it is rather boring.

The gurus are also keen on examining the 'fundamentals' of a company. They recommend really hard research on things like assets, value, growth, profit-and-loss accounts, debt, dividend yield, market capitalisation and the price-to-earnings ratio. Now a study of all these worthy matters is a very sensible thing to do. I try to study them myself and advise you to.

But you won't find many technical bits in this book. Nor any of the usual jargon. The tips here are simple and easy to understand. Most are based on pop psychology and common sense. Even so, *Armchair Tycoon* is not meant as a substitute for painstaking research into any companies you invest in. You should always do your homework.

Another thing you may notice about this ripping collection is that a few of the investment hints seem to contradict each other. This is inevitable when you gather together a galaxy of ideas from an army of City professionals, all with different personalities and methods. This is just one reason why you should never act on one tip only. Treat each piece of advice as just one of many pointers, before you buy or sell a share. Don't act unless several of the hints apply.

I've begun with a few dollops of general advice which is meant as a safety first exercise. You probably want to hear what to do rather than what not to do, but share investment is a serious matter, and this is a responsible book. So it's perhaps best to start in this way. I don't want anyone to get hurt.

One more thing. View all your share dealing as an enjoyable hobby. You may not feel like having a romp and frolic in the woods when one of your selections dives, dives, dives. . . but force yourself to take the brighter view of share-picking. This book will make your trading enjoyable. I would be surprised if it didn't make you richer, too.

Ground Rules

You can try starting a successful share-picking career by simply dialling a broker and buying into a few companies at random. But it won't work. You stand a better chance of erecting Westminster Abbey by tossing a mountain of stones on the site without benefit of an architect's plan. Those investors who make millions out of shares all have a grand design. It's made up of rules, some of which they bend, some they never tinker with. So let's start with some classic dictums of lucrative share trading which should not be broken.

Be Different

Ineffectual investors follow the herd. The crowd may be right some of the time, as they're all following the same obvious pointers to success. But if everybody is correct about a situation, and puts their mouth where everybody else's is, profits won't be worth hollering about. It's a bit like everyone being guided by current form to pick draws on a football coupon. If the chosen teams all draw, everyone wins the pools, but the cash prizes are laughable. It's only by being right when most folk are up the creek that you can ever hope to win enough for a private island, a Rolls Royce and a small jet.

It usually pays to buy shares when the market is at the bottom of a bad patch. This is when most bargains are found. You would expect everybody to realise this, but many investors do the exact opposite. You see, it's hard to buy when share prices are falling like ninepins, as it shows everybody else is selling. It's a hostile climate for buying. When your lift suddenly dives down five floors, you can't expect it to shoot upwards again. But while plunging lifts don't usually bounce back, shares nearly always do. So if you buy equities when they're at their lowest ebb, you get lots more for your money and can sell them back when the market picks up.

Now take the opposite case. The FTSE 100 (or Footsie) the famous index of shares in Britain's top companies, is at an all-time high. Everything in the garden is rosy. You missed the boat earlier but the happy atmosphere in the City is intoxicating and you expect the Footsie to scale even greater heights. So you buy shares in a few blue-chip companies when they have never been so expensive. This is a mistake, as money markets rarely travel in straight lines. After breaking a record, they take a rest, then usually stagger backwards quite a way, exhausted by their earlier efforts.

SUCCESS
THIS WAY

FOLLOW THE
POINTERS &
THE HERD

Smarter investors know that it's wiser to buy when others are glum about the market's future prospects, not when their expectations are soaring. And when everybody else is feeling bullish (City speak for optimistic), they put their hands in their pockets – and keep them there.

If you heed this advice – to buy when the stock market is floundering and sell when it's blooming – you will be following a principle which has made people rich throughout history: 'Buy cheap and sell dear'.

However, the stock market, being less reliable than a scorpion in a bran tub, doesn't always follow the normal paths of commerce. The stock you sell 'dear' may climb bigger peaks after you sold it, while the shares you bought 'cheap' may become cheaper still. In other words, you may end up selling all your best shares to be left with a load of rubbish. What you need is a few pointers as to when a share is really at the top and when it's at its final bottom. We'll look at some of these valuable signals later on.

Look for a Happening

Shares may rise and fall with the market as a whole. But they won't outdo the field unless something happens to the company issuing them. In the City, this is known as 'a story'. It could be a new product, a hefty order, new laws, a change of boss, a take-over (real or rumoured) or any combination of these. The smaller the firm, the bigger waves you can expect the change to make. If such an event happens to a grand company, there'll be heavy press coverage and you probably won't beat City professionals in the rush to buy shares before they take off. But if you spot a minor news item on something exceptional happening to a fly-weight, you might have a chance to nip in and buy a stake while the shares are still at their old price.

Sources

When I was a cub reporter, I was told to find two separate sources for a big story – and three for a truly controversial piece. Just one person may have been enough to tell us about a duck-shaped potato, but we weren't allowed into print with a story of significance unless a pair of different individuals confirmed the facts first. Many of the fiscal wizards who've provided hints for this book, have adapted this traditional newspaper policy to their share trading. They'll cold-shoulder any company until they've had sunny reports from at least three directions – a newspaper, analyst, stockbroker, tip sheet, respected friend or whatever – that the enterprise is going places. Most key investors will also expect a company they're contemplating to have at least three 'hot properties' classically linked with sure-fire success. This could be an electric management, a thumping good product and low prices. Or it could have big cash reserves, little or no debt and a popular brand image. It may also boast three entirely different positive features. But it's not enough for a firm to have just one good thing going for it – it needs to have at least three.

How Much to Spend on Shares

Even brokers, who need your business to survive, will tell you only to invest what you can spare. But my advice is to be even more cautious than that. Only invest what you can afford to lose without missing it if you lose the lot. There are two ways to 'miss' money – either practically or philosophically. You can miss it in the sense that it affects your standard of living. Or you can miss it, not because you can't afford the loss, but because it preys on your mind. Those of thrifty tendencies will know that the 'philosophical' kind of loss can be just as devastating as the first.

Even if, as a would-be investor, you decide that you can afford to try shares because your way of life won't be jeopardised, you must still consider another personal resource – and that's your temperament. Do you have the right sort of personality to invest in equities? Will you smart, fume and fret for years if you lose money or can you happily forget all about it? There's no point in share-picking if it brings you pain. You wouldn't go wind-surfing if you were worried sick about hypothermia or being eaten by sharks. So if you're going to lose sleep over money lost in the turbulent world of shares give this book to a charity shop and stay clear.

Good Target Practice

Greed is an ugly word. Most of us deny we're guilty. Most of us are. Those who say the stock market is entirely driven by fear and greed are right. Financial gluttony is the devil behind our shoulder when we try to make more cash out of a thrilling development on the stock market than it's reasonable to expect. Here's an example. Cucumber Holdings Ltd has announced a merger with The Sandwich Corporation. Cucumber shares, which you hold, start rising sharply. They soar 40p the first day, 30p on the second and there's a 10p improvement on the third. Now the action slows into a see-saw movement, with the price alternating between 2p up and 2p down, over a week. Then there's a 10p slip. The temptation is to ignore this fall and hang on to your shares in case they rise further. But if you don't sell now, the shares may soon slump to their original level. Yet the temptation to keep your shares for a bit longer – fuelled by greed – can be overowering.

How can you fight the urge not to sell when all the omens say the share is as high as it's going to be for quite some time? Well, some of the best investors use fixed 'targets'. They work like this. Bill knows that mergers, like that of Cucumber Holdings and The Sandwich Corporation, are pretty common. He's been watching the behaviour of shares in similar situations for years. This experience helps him to guess how far the price for Cucumber shares will push up before they sink again. He decides on this price. When the share attains that level he sells his holding. There's no argument about it. A trade is definitely made. Of course, even for an old stager like Bill, temptation kicks in when his target price is reached. He's bound to think: 'Maybe if I just leave it another couple of days, I should be able to get at least another few pence a share.' You might call this kind of brinkmanship being brave. But really, it's a demonstration of weak will, akin to breaking a New Year resolution.

Actually, there is an easy way of sticking to a target which doesn't leave you with the awful decision of whether to break a promise to yourself. If you choose this method, the target will be kept and the shares sold without any action on your part. All you need do, as soon as the merger is announced, is to instruct a broker to sell once the share reaches your magic level. He won't expect another phone call before acting on his volition, not yours. This takes away the burden of indecision. It also helps you to feel less sick than a parrot when the rotten shares climb another 50p past your target figure.

If you have recently taken a profit on a share which then went on to break further ground, it may console you to learn that in my long experience of share dealing neither I, nor anybody I know, has ever sold shares exactly at the top of the 'high-low' curve. Nor have I managed to buy a share at the very bottom.

Stop Losses

These are the opposite of high targets. You decide, when buying a share, exactly how much you're prepared to see it fall in value before you let go. This is your 'stop loss'. When it reaches that level, you don't wait for a possible bounce-back, you act firmly, take your money and run. Stop losses prevent you fretting too much if things start to go wrong. It's not entirely foolproof as the company in question could be suspended unexpectedly on the Stock Exchange before your low point is reached. But normally stop losses do limit the damage very effectively. And remember that many experts believe that avoiding heavy losses is more important to their final wealth tally than picking out winners.

But on what level should a stop loss be safely set? This is a tricky choice. It depends on many things. If you've done marvellously with your trading overall, you can afford to take more chances and set your cut-off limit rather low. If the share is prone to wild up-

and-down swings you should also fix your limit lower than you might do with a more stable company. Penny share companies also deserve a lower stop loss. If you had hoped to make a quick profit within a few weeks of buying the share, and this hasn't happened, you probably need a higher stop loss. Some analysts stick to the same cut-off point in all circumstances. It's usually 20 per cent for an average equity or 30 per cent for a really volatile share.

All share management systems have variations. A popular modification to the stop-loss ploy appeals to investors who can't trust their ability to live without regret. They use a stop loss limit, but apply it to only half their holding. This enables them to have their cake and eat it, or at least to have half their cake and eat half of it. The advantage here is that you won't lose so much cash if the company gets into real trouble, but you still have an interest in the race after the stop limit is breached. The latter benefit comes in very handy if a share suddenly rockets away from its customary position of bumping along the bottom.

Stop losses can also be useful when it comes to selling a winning share. You allow the rising share to drag a 20 per cent cut-off point behind it. For example, if a share improves from £1 to £2, your stop loss rises with it to £1.60, instead of the previous 80p. So you would now sell your share if it slips from £2 to £1.60.

Readies at the Ready

Old hands will tell you never to put all your money into shares. Keep some cash standing by in your current account. Then if you need a big sum for a holiday, say, or a home extension you won't have to sell equities to raise it. If you don't have cash standing by, you may be forced to hurriedly trade in a holding which is still pregnant with profitable possibilities. You will also need spare funds to pay for shares if a gilded opportunity knocks unexpectedly.

Some investors arrange an overdraft facility to pay for any unexpected share opportunities, but I don't advise it. Keeping some of your portfolio in cash also hedges your bets if a market crash comes along.

All right, that's a few basic principles to bear in mind in all your share dealings. And now that we've given you a few useful hints to stop you falling on your face, let's take a look at the way some shares fall into pigeon-holes. If they stay in these easily-recognised categories for some time, it helps to predict how shares may behave in coming months – and telling the future is what every investor fantasises about . . .

Share Categories

Shares are like stars in the heavens. Some become black holes into which our money vanishes never to be seen again. Others are shooting stars, rising far and fast. And you find pulsar shares which alternate between shining brightly and fading away. As well as falling sometimes or going supernova, shares, like celestial beacons, can light up our lives.

Like heavenly bodies, shares can also be lumped into categories which behave in a recognisable fashion. The difference is that shares, unlike stars, can flit in and out of different classifications at will. So we never know for certain whether they'll continue performing in a certain way or alter their behaviour completely. Or if this change is to be temporary on permanent.

All shares which have demonstrated certain characteristics now and in the recent past cannot be guaranteed to behave that way for many more months or even the next few minutes. Having said that, it will be helpful to know what the various categories of shares are, so that if the stock of a company you fancy begins to behave in a certain way it will give you some idea of how it might perform later. Let's look at some of the more promising categories which some shares fit into.

Yo-Yo's

This type of share has proved a money spinner for me over the years. It has given me a profit of around 10 per cent on an average of twice every 12 months. The yo-yo share bounces up and down between low and high levels which seem pretty fixed. It's like an abandoned boat bumping between the upper and lower banks of a river. Typically, the price rarely drops below £5 and has yet to rise beyond £5.50. The obvious strategy is to buy when the share is at its nadir and get rid at the top of its usual band.

This is easier said than done. Otherwise all yo-yo fans would be rich. But once you've identified the usual highs and lows, the chances of making a profit are increased.

It's not a good idea to wait for the £5.50 target every time before selling. The best plan is to wait for a steady ascent of around 3p or 4p a day towards the target. If the share steadies and drops a few pence before it quite reaches the top, then ring your broker to make a disposal. You know the share has never yet broken through £5.50, so it's best to be cautious and cash your chips before the target.

What kind of share becomes a yo-yo, rather than acting more conventionally? That's to say rising and falling fairly steadily in one direction, give or take the odd correction along the way. Well, a yo-yo is usually quite pricey: between £5 and £10 is representative. It's sometimes a big company, even a blue chip. The Footsie index of Britain's 100 top companies includes some yo-yo giants.

Prices tend to travel up and down between their two fairly fixed buffers if some kind of cloud has been hanging over the company for a long time. Examples might be: a big project held up by planning inquiries, rumours about a new kind of tax or a monopoly inquiry.

Why should such a situation cause the company's market value to become lodged in an up-and-down limbo? Well, one theory implicates financial journalists. A press commentator is stuck for a new story. So he returns to a familiar one about a big company which is going through the wringer (City talk for experiencing all sorts of problems). They'll look at the old facts and try to put an even worse slant on them to make an interesting read. Other journalists adapt this 'new' story for their own columns.

Readers who hold shares are discouraged by what they interpret as a new downturn in their company's fortunes. They sell and the share price falls. The value continues its descent until bargain-hunters, more informed than average share holders, step in. The price heads north again. Shareholders regain confidence. More shares are sold, making up lost ground. Then, by the time the share approaches its usual roof, another journalist is stuck for a story . . .

To spot a yo-yo, check the highest and lowest prices of big companies in the financial pages. Then keep a watch on Teletext and Ceefax to see if the shares oscillate between the two points. It's worth the effort of identifying such a company as you could net a premium twice a year – or more if the share has lots of mood swings.

However each profit isn't likely to be massive on a modest holding of shares. This is because the up and down limits aren't usually too far apart. And taking just two profits a year will entail four trades involving dealing costs.

The Roller Coaster

Though related to the yo-yo this division of share goes up and down at the speed of light. It doesn't do anything special for years. Then it suddenly swings around wildly for months at a time. It's a little harder to be sure when to buy and sell, because its outer limits aren't as firm as the yo-yo. But it can show faster profits.

The roller coaster share often turns up on the daily listings of the biggest winners and losers on TV text pages. For a day or two it sits happily in the 'winners' column. Next day a fall follows pride – and it's among the 'losers'.

This unstable state can come about if the company concerned has struck a giant deal with an entrepreneur or another firm. The City has trouble deciding if the link-up is likely to work. Confidence surges and ebbs – and so does the share price.

A short watch on levels will help you decide on the best price to sell and the best to buy. The difference between the two (it's known as the channel) is often wide enough for your broker's cut not to deter you from doing quite a few trades while the action lasts. This can be all over in a few months, but has been known to last longer.

Buying a roller coaster is fun because there's nearly always something happening to it. For the same reason you must keep track of the share every day to earn a chance of profiting from the ride.

Baby Walkers

These are shares which rise slowly and regularly in even steps. Sometimes there's an occasional wobble, but the line of ascendancy is more or less straight. They scale quite a peak, then begin a stately progression back down again. Back at base, the journey begins all over again. These tours continue, more or less within the same high and low parameters for a year, sometimes more. If you chase the history back, you may find a major slice of good news which triggered the cycle. It could be a huge deal which gave the share a quick fillip. City analysts take a few days to digest the news and may add more fuel to the fire. Then those speculators who always chase a rising share, without bothering to research its form and real prospects, start to pile in. The share really takes off, reaching heights which are unjustified by the original news. But this defiance of gravity doesn't last and the shares trundle back to earth.

Over-Reactors

These are shares which are out of kilter with the *Financial Times* All Share Index. The index goes up or down depending on the adventures of the general economy. Over-reactor shares follow the average trend of other shares in the index, but when the index rises, an over-reactor climbs even more. And when the index falls, it dismays its backers by toppling even further.

One way to pick out an over-reactor is to keep an eye on the biggest winner and loser pages on Ceefax. Some companies appear in both lists over time more often than others. These may well be over-reactors (though how long they might remain in this class isn't certain).

Once they've spotted an over-reactor how do investors hope to make money out of it? Well, if all their research indicates the stock market is entering a boom, they might buy this kind of share, expecting it to rise more than the average stock. But if the market shows signs of retreating, you might sell an over-reactor as it could fall lower than average.

Defensive Shares

These are shares which historically have risen and fallen less than most equities during dramatic changes on the stock market. If the index rises, you would possibly not want to own them, but if you think the market is about to suffer, you might switch into them as a way of limiting any losses. Defensive shares are a bit harder to identify as you can't use the 'big winners and losers' columns. But it is possible to pick them out over a period of time by consulting share price lists. Do they move about much when the index does, or do they shift less than you'd expect? One test might be if the index improves by two per cent, does the individual share rise by the same percentage of its value? If it rises by only one per cent – and there's been no obvious news to depress the share – then it is probably a defensive share.

Rising Stars

To do well with this share needs a fairly close eye on financial pages. But your vigilance may be worth it as any profit may come quickly. You search out an equity which has been unobtrusively rising a few pennies over two days. Yet there are no accompanying stories in the papers saying why this should be. Obviously something is going on, but it doesn't seem to be public knowledge yet. (You may have missed something, because you can't read everything. But this probably means others didn't spot it either.)

If only a few people know where the rising star gets its new driving force, there may be no sudden rushes upwards. But the ride may continue for several more days yet. What should you do? You'd like to jump on a bandwagon which is passing through such lush scenery, but you know it's gambling to act blind. But then you do know something about the share: that other punters are confident to put money in daily. Some investors think it is worth buying into a rising star because when news of the mysterious development which may be nudging it upwards becomes generally known there may be a big one-day leap.

But what if there is no hidden factor? Suppose the share was only improving daily because many other investors thought there was. Does it help to remind you that some folk believe that where there's smoke there's fire?

Fallen Angels

The following tip has been confided in me by many successful investors and comes highly recommended. Fallen angels are big companies which have stumbled on rocky ground. Their share values have behaved like a stone in a well after bad news, a profit warning say, and have continued to plummet. They're well worth watching for signs of a recovery. Because after a year or two in the doldrums, fallen angels can shoot skywards again in a spectacular way.

Why should they? After all many smaller firms which fall from orbit burn up in an unforgiving atmosphere never to be seen again. Well, corporations big enough to be household names usually have the best paid leaders on the board. Most of their directors are business wizards of the highest category. They may have made misjudgements, but more likely their company fortunes have been blasted by ill-luck. Perhaps world economics or currency changes have swung against them.

Top directors smart with failure more than lesser souls. They yearn to be back on top. They also have the talent and experience to learn from mistakes fast and do something about them. Despite its set-backs, the company will have resources enough to bring in even more gifted experts to bolster a recovery operation. Members of the beleaguered board may also begin working 16 hours a day to restore their company fortunes and their reputations. They'll make huge efforts to secure giant foreign orders. They want the world to know that they're succeeding again so publicity will be courted like there's no tomorrow. All this should bring investors back by the coach-load.

There are other reasons why fallen angels often don't stay in the mire long. Sometimes the product is so prestigious, aeroplanes or cars, say, that the government is horrified at the effect of such a prominent bankruptcy on world confidence in Britain. They may also worry about an immense toll on jobs. Ministers may agree loans, or even grants to keep the concern afloat. And as long as you're afloat you can be rescued.

The snag, as always, is to guess when the company has arrested its descent and is about to haul back. It's no easy decision because fallen angels can topple further than you'd expect. Blame the institutions for this. Fund managers for pension firms, unit trusts and insurance giants buy heavily into blue-chip companies because they know they're comparatively safe. They can also conveniently buy their shares in huge blocks.

But managers of large funds can be pretty disloyal when signs of trouble appear – and are indecently quick to start severing connections. This causes the price to fall further. The more it decays, the more big investors divest themselves causing an avalanche. Soon the share value has tumbled way below its fair level. And just when you think the worst is over, there's another flurry of falling snow.

So it's probably better to wait a few weeks until things have settled before putting money in. This could be when the share price has been static for at least a week or better still when it begins rising a few pence over some days. Experienced investors always tell me that it often pays to wait longer than your natural instinct dictates. They argue that 'a lost opportunity is better than an actual loss'.

The recovery when it comes for a large company, can be impressive. Many rise well over their level before the fall – and in pretty quick time. This is because those fickle institutions start buying back in again and a new rush starts – to pour money back in. Two examples of companies which have done this in the past are British Aerospace and the old British Gas.

A fallen angel back in favour is a share which many investors like to put away in their bottom drawer rather than desert for quick profits. Once the cold wind of near-failure has blown away the dross, the company should be leaner, fitter and stronger. It will have learned the hard way. The chastened directors could continue raking in new orders and trimming operating expenses for many years, shining a steadily burning light on thousands of portfolios.

The Nine-Day Wonder

We all know that even the juiciest news items stay in the public imagination for just over a week. It's the same with equities. A real development or an unfounded rumour sends a share upwards. It improves consistently as the news is digested by the City and its followers. Some folk act fast, others dither. And just like a sleazy political scandal or a showbiz sensation, after nine-days, interest suddenly evaporates. The steady rise now falters and wanes. After two or three weeks, the price may be back where it started. Some investors build the nine-day wonder phenomenon into their buy-or-sell calculations. The advice from my City informants is to sell after an eight-day steady plod upwards.

If the news story sends some of your existing shares into free-fall, sell on day one and buy back on the eighth day. Hopefully the share will begin a rebound once the negative story has faded from the collective mind. However if the story was quite damning, you might decide not to repurchase after your early sale.

Stagnant Pools

I've bought cheap shares in a small company, only to see them sink even lower. Stupidly anxious to save face, I can't bring myself to cut my losses. Many more like me refuse to sell. But nobody else wants to buy such a no-hoper. So the price stays on its same miserable level for a year or longer. But what's this? Suddenly the share starts to wobble and hesitantly leaves the sea bottom. Once this process starts the rise can be rapid, sometimes reaching a five-fold improvement within a week. The sea-change may be because a new seriously rich investor has piled in or there may be word of vastly improved profits. But who cares – the share's rising.

What should you do – if anything – and when should you do it? You could come out fairly quickly in case of a relapse. You might wait for your stake to double before ringing your broker. You could be braver, keeping a close eye on the share listings, hoping to scoop a windfall when the action stops. Or you can take an even more courageous course and invest yet more cash before the phoenix finishes its miraculous upward journey. Whatever you do, act fast. This kind of thing often starts and finishes inside a week. One reason why the action is short-lived is that most people watching the share are early investors like yourself. They've previously taken a pounding. So they're extra nervous. They're prepared to put in more cash to offset previous losses, but they're prone to sell like lightning once the share starts to wobble.

It's because stagnant pool shares are occasionally refreshed by new life springs that I sometimes feel justified in allowing them to moulder in my portfolio for years. Some stockbrokers scorn this kind of inaction. You should, they say, never sit on your losses. But with very small companies, I've found it occasionally pays (though the danger of complete collapse is always there). However, once a newly-revived firm has reached a new level, it can start falling again. Sometimes this beastly process takes a longish time, but it's not uncommon.

Steady Risers

These tend to be shares in fairly unknown firms. As they're not in the public eye nobody notices a penny or two improvement almost daily. Something is obviously going on, but the press have bigger fish to fry. So no articles appear to explain the phenomenon. Could it be that a big investor is buying stock only gradually to stop the rest of us noticing? Is a bid in the offing? Or is the company nearing annual report day when appetising profits will be announced?

Does it really matter what the reason is? There's doubtless a very good underlying reason for the slow but sure increase, so you could join the bandwagon. The reason will probably become clear very soon – at which time there may be an even bigger jump in price for you to take advantage of. If the secret force behind the ascent never becomes clear, then you should sell on the day after the share grinds to a halt.

Of course, it makes sense to try to find the reason. But don't ring a city editor. You may tip him off to a story which might start a flood of investment before you could buy. You might try to discover the name of the registrar from your broker and ask them if they have any news to explain the rise.

Falling Rocks

Unsettling news slices a few pennies off a share's value. Really bad news sends them on a journey to the centre of the Earth. It's not unusual for some firms to lose half their asset value within a few hours, if not minutes. A common cause of such disaster is the frightful profit warning. This is when a company admits, as it's compelled to do, that its results, to be announced later, will make shareholders bay for blood. When the profit warning is sounded, many investors, especially the institutions, unload as fast as they can. Like a run on the bank, once this process starts, it's hard to stop.

It doesn't take long for the stricken share to pull out of the dive, although its new level will be well down. But in life, what falls fast on to a floor often rebounds. And this is true of the Stock Exchange. In fact, many shares in this situation act like a bungee jumper. They bounce, rising to a new level, though not as high as the original. Then they keel over backwards again, but not tumbling as low as they did earlier, and so on.

I usually wait two days after a profit warning has done its evil work, then I buy in. As I'm not the only 'rescuer', the price may rise again at this point. This can be a gradual climb, but often it's an enthusiastic jump. Some punters leave their money in, hoping the correction will be long-lasting. But I pull out at the first sign of wobble. I am rather cowardly.

After all, a profit warning, if that caused the problem, has to be regarded seriously. If the previous share price was not so much based on past performance as linked to future expectations, then it was woefully over-valued. A drop in profits might mean the product or service on offer has outlived its usefulness. That could only make things worse in future years. Perhaps the company is overwhelmed by competition from abroad. Perhaps a director has blessed a tropical paradise with company funds. Whatever the cause, the money coming in is down – and earnings are everything.

It's hard to live down a profits warning. It puts a brake on investors and it discourages take-over bids. This means that the price may fall even further in the weeks after the 'bungee jumping' settles down. So after the first bounce, many investors sell. And the few times I've not taken early profits, greedily waiting for something better, I've ended up nurturing a loss.

But I'm not complaining. There is reason not to be dismayed by profit warnings. Top investors look forward to profit warnings (if they don't already have a holding), as a good healthy twang back can turn a fast buck.

Falling rock shares can plunge for reasons other than a profit warning. A suspected fraud may be admitted or the directors fall out. If Teletext or Ceefax don't give the reason for the decline as a profit warning, stay clear. If dirty work is afoot, a more useful thing to do with your cash is to stand in a park hurling tenners to the wind.

Snakes and Ladders

Though shares which sometimes find themselves in the snakes and ladders category are pretty common, opportunities to make money from them are fairly rare. The trouble is that their high and low levels are even harder than usual to predict. Though they do move within a fairly predictable channel. (This is the City name for the normal path of a share with the high price at the top and the lowest price at the bottom.)

As you'd expect, snakes and ladders shares ascend on slow but sure 'ladders', until they unexpectedly hit a 'snake'. This could be a set of poor results posted by another, but similar firm, or perhaps a change in law which slows business. The share falls down the snake a lot faster than it rose and can languish there for some time. The answer is not to be greedy. When the ladder climbing improves a share by something substantial like 10p or it continues over two weeks, take profits. Or keep the share for ever and hope there are more ladders than snakes.

Triangles

This is a difficult category of share to recognise because it conforms to a pattern which isn't apparent at first glance. You need to know a share's recent history – and to have a pencil and paper. Draw two lines at right angles. Mark the upright stem of the right angle 'price' and the horizontal line 'time'. Indicate the weekly high and low prices of a share by a series of dots. Then join the dots up with a ruler. If the highs and lows have become less pronounced in time then the two lines should come together to form a triangle with its sharp angle to the right of your graph. This is considered to be a good sign for the share's future performance.

If the business of drawing the diagram above doesn't appeal, you can make a guess as to whether a share falls into triangle mode by looking at its highs and lows over six months. If the tops and bottoms are gradually becoming less far apart then you've probably spotted a triangle share.

That's a selection of some of the classifications into which shares can fall. But remember that the shares which fall into these 'pigeon-holes' may not remain there for long. Stocks which rise up and down in a prescribed fashion for a time, may switch out of the category without warning and perform quite differently. For the unwary this can bring disaster. Always be on guard for a share which suddenly jumps out of its usual classification and begins to behave oddly.

Tactics

To be a flourishing investor you need to be a few steps ahead of the majority. One way of sprinting up the staircase of opportunity (sounds like an Eddie Cochran song) is to have a fistful of wheezes that are regular servants of top money-makers in the share world. Here are some of them.

Do-the-Same-Game

A high street chain announces unexpectedly good results. Suddenly, the City expects most big stores in the land to have been making money at the same rate. With the speed of light, shares in companies all over the retail sector are marked up. But it's the reporting company's more obvious rivals which are most affected by this frenzy. Those stores not in the same league are largely untouched by the news. Big institutional buyers are the ones who react to developments like this and they're only concerned with large firms. It may take a few days for the implications of those higher profits of the famous store chain to filter down to the smaller shopping outlets. This is a big advantage to the nippy private investor. He may have a chance to get in just before shares in smaller retailers also go up.

A word of warning, though. The chances are that if one store announces big profits, then the public may indeed have been spending freely in shops everywhere. But don't trust a small shop chain with your life savings – until you've checked with your own eyes that its branch in your locality is usually choked with customers.

Should a famous chain own up to a big drop in profits, you may want to rapidly divest yourself of any shares you hold in the retail sector, as consumer spending may be suffering universally. On the other hand, you may have a low opinion of the store group with collapsed profits. In which case other investors will too – and the damage to profits will be confined to that one business.

Bargain Hunting

It's lucky that all's fair in love and stock markets. Otherwise the time-honoured custom of bargain hunting might be sneered at as a blatant attempt to profit from somebody else's misfortune. It's a

very common strategy, undertaken by some investors to the point of obsession. Anyone who doubts that should keep an eye on the 'Winners and Losers' page on Ceefax or Teletext. Note the progress of shares in a company which has just announced a 'profits warning'. After a day or two of heavy falls, there's a bounce back of some sort, the share price recovering some ground. The most common reason given on the screen for a rebound is: 'bargain hunting'. This familiar explanation for a dramatic rebound after a nasty fall is offered time and time again.

There are two kinds of bargain hunter – the automatic and the informed. The auto hunter quickly spots a share's sudden fall from grace. She waits a few days until the regression seems complete. The shares now being much cheaper than they were, she feels confident enough to start mopping them up. She calculates that the big sellers over-reacted earlier in the week and that shares she now owns will soon approach their former level. Then she can sell them again. She assumes that what goes down must come up.

The other kind of bargain hunter, the 'informed' type, also aims to profit from a sudden disaster. She, too, hopes the bad news will bring down the price of a share to a much lower level. But before she buys stricken shares, she takes a few precautions. She checks if the company has enough 'value' to propel it skywards again, despite the recent set-back. Included in his list of questions are: does the concern have resilient managers, does it have big cash reserves, does the share price reflect the value of assets and are there bags of debt to pay off? This information will show whether the shares were 'toppy' (City slang for over-priced) when they fell and deserved to be hauled back, or if they were fairly priced at the time of the fall, and will soon snap back to their former glory. If the search is favourable, the 'informed bargain-hunter' will buy the ill-fated stock.

Playing with Big Boys

If you read that banks, insurance giants, and pension funds are buying into one particular domain of business, it should give you confidence to follow suit. You wouldn't believe how much big institutions pay gifted researchers to check the financial status, products and prospects of businesses before they plough millions into them. If you discover that one particular company is specially favoured by the pros, you should take even more notice. After all, this is a rare opportunity to benefit from top quality, astronomically-expensive, commercial analysis for nothing.

Even so, as with most of the tips in this book, it's best not to rely solely on a view favoured by the big institutions when choosing stock. After all, when was any expert always right! Wait for other pieces of information about a target company to come your way before you 'take a position'. (This is a posh term for buying shares and is very useful for impressing friends.)

Smart Money Play

In your Sunday paper you see an article saying all the 'smart money' is going into Such and Such Ltd. I've never found anybody who knows exactly what 'smart money' is, but if it's cash belonging to very intelligent City types, then you might be inclined to give the company a bit of a spin. This is not necessarily because you believe in the 'smartness' of the money in question but that 'a lot of it' is going into Such and Such Ltd, doing wonders for its share price. Be ready to beat a hasty retreat though.

Bandwagoning

You've been hearing a lot about a new company in the telephone business. In fact, every time you pick up a newspaper, there's another snippet about the venture. Nothing bad, you know, just items about a new technology, a fresh deal or a whiz kid manager brought in. The new firm is mentioned a few times on the radio and its adverts look impressive on the telly. Its newly-launched shares are picking up a few pence every day. Should you join in the rush? Do you sniff a gold rush? Perhaps.

Ploughing money into a new undertaking which attracts a deal of publicity is often a good idea, because a lot of trumpet-blowing by journalists attracts share buyers just as TV advertising sucks in new customers. But you need to be in early, well before the bally-hoo starts to die down. You should also be prepared to sell at the drop of a hat if your shares go into reverse. This is because a new venture rarely goes straight into profit. Any gains may not show on the balance sheet for years to come. Nobody knows what future profits will be. If any bad news rises to the surface in a sea of media euphoria, then all the work of press relations people in stoking up the share price will be undone. That's because there's no history of profit-making to support the price. So my team of advisors say: take advantage of the big build-up – but be ready to come out quickly. Perhaps the firm will go on to become as big as BT, but you can always climb back aboard once its future is more assured.

Chasing Down

This stratagem is a bit hair-raising: only for the strong-nerved who can afford to lose a lot of money if the plan goes pear-shaped. Some leading investors I consulted for this book went white around the gills at the mere mention of chasing down, believing it to be too hazardous. Please be warned that those of a nervous disposition should skip to the next section. Why the concern? Well, chasing down has been likened to the gambling system known as 'doubling-up' (though it's not nearly as senseless). This is how doubling-up works on a roulette wheel. You stake one chip on the red, but the ball settles in a black pocket on the wheel. Next time, you put two chips on red. If it comes up, you gain two chips so cancelling out your previous loss. But if black turns up again, you will need to put four chips on the red for a third spin to break even. You know that red will come up *sometime* so you keep backing it, but your quantity

of chips has to double each time to get all your stake back. You don't have to be a mathematician to know that if red doesn't show for some time, you are in dead trouble!

But it's unfair to compare doubling-up with chasing down shares because in a chase down you don't double your stake each time. The similarity is that both systems involve running after your losses. For example, you invest £500 in the Cauliflower Estates. But things go wrong and in six months' time the initial price of £1 per share now stands at 50p. You confer with all the oracles you can – the balance sheets, press reports, tip sheets, your broker and so on. Though there are minor reasons why the share halved, you're still confident that Cauliflower Estates has prospects for a recovery. Having done this homework, followers of the chase down principle will now match their original stake with an additional investment of £500. This time, instead of taking charge of 500 shares, they buy twice as many for the same money. They now have a total of 1,500 shares.

If the investor hadn't taken this second bite at the cherry, the share price would need to rise 50p to recoup his £500 outlay. By risking another £500, the share price only has to rise 25p for him to get back the total of both investments. The share is, of course, more likely to rise by 25p than 50p. And if the share does leap by another 50p, then the investor won't just break even, he'll make a handsome profit.

By deploying the chase down, you expose yourself (not literally, please!) to any further relapse in the share price. If it tumbles again, a brave investor – after re-checking the company's financial credentials – might deliver a third injection of £500. This time Cauliflower Estates equities may have sunk to 25p each, so he's now able to snap up another 2,000 shares. Now he needs an even smaller rise in the share price to get all his £1,500 back. But the price might tumble yet again – and the expensive process could go on until the darned company finally disappears from view.

A sensible share-picker would only make the second investment. If the price lurched downwards again, he should cut his losses and sell, rather than hazard any more cash. Unless, that is, he discovers really good reasons to believe a third try will finally do the trick. And even then he might reduce the size of the stake.

A strength of the chase down is that you recognised 'good value' when you first bought the shares. When they halved in price, it's probable that, even despite the bad news which sent them falling, they represented an even better bargain at 50p each. And, having lived through a bad patch, you might expect the worst to be over. I have 'chased down' from time to time, though never beyond a second investment. Sometimes I came unstuck. I also once hesitated to use the system after seeing a penny share slip from 12p to 3p over two years. Then I watched in horror as it rose from 3p to 18p in four weeks and, a few weeks later, gained another 3p. If I had bought more shares at 3p, I would have made a killing. But I understand why I didn't act. The share had fallen too far for comfort and spectacular recoveries like this are rare.

Using the chase down flies in the face of the analyst's classic advice to cut your losses after a 20 per cent fall and don't look back. And there's an uncomfortable psychological snag, too. It's very cruel to the nerves to invest more than once in a company which has failed you; it smacks uncomfortably of hurling good money after bad. So look hard before you leap – and know when to stop leaping altogether.

The Fast Turn

This is a basic device which makes more sense if you're a big spender. It only really pays if you can order shares in big clumps. All you do is buy into a company in which you're led to believe (through press reports, usually) that something dramatic is about to happen. This might be a deal, a take-over, a famous new chief executive or whatever. If nothing does transpire, and the shares are moribund for more than four weeks, get out. Be steely about this – four weeks only! This will free your money up for another, more worthwhile investment.

The fast turn isn't cost effective if you only take a few shares. You will have to pay two sets of dealing commissions which are more expensive if you buy in small bundles. And critics of the fast turn will remind you of Sod's Law. That much vaunted event on which you pinned your hopes, will almost certainly come to pass only moments after the shares are sold. In the share world, patience likes to get her own back on those who snub her.

Timing

Every success story owes something to good timing. It's probably just as important as knowledge and more vital than luck in getting what you want in life. Choosing the exact moment to pounce is particularly pertinent in share dealing. It's also much harder to get it right, and is naturally more crucial for rapid in-and-out trading than it is when investing over a long period.

One interesting aspect of timing is knowing when it's best to buy or sell at different points during the stock market day. Anything can happen between 8.30am and 4.30pm. But if you watch changing share prices carefully, you may reach two conclusions: firstly, some hours can be more hectic than others; secondly, 'buy' and 'sell' trades should be made at different times of the day. These findings conform to a rule I made up, but which sounds like an important scientific law: 'Humans taken in quantity all take similar courses of action at the same time, most of the time.' This, of course, is a description of the herd instinct.

We all have mood swings. These are affected by meals. Most of us have breakfast, lunch and dinner at roughly the same time. The weather also works on moods. Everybody in the same place has the same sunshine or cloud. Fund managers for City institutions, who really drive the markets, all work the same office hours in similar office environs. This means that they are all likely to be active at similar times during the day and rather lethargic at others.

How does this mass psychology affect you? Well, imagine one of your shares is rising rather fitfully. You plan to sell the holding today because the chances are that current enthusiasm will cool overnight and profit-takers will start some heavy selling tomorrow. You obviously need to know the best time to sell today.

I've been watching price changes on both the main TV text services every working day for the last seven years. While I've kept no records, I believe I can risk some educated guesses at the rough times when prices are most likely to rise and fall (not counting sudden market swings). These impressions have been supported, albeit a bit grudgingly, by City journalists and stockbrokers. Here then is how shares tend to rise or fall during one trading session.

Very often, a share starts the day as it means to go on. So let's look at a share which starts the session a few pence up on yesterday's final price. From this promising start, it will often crawl upwards in fits and starts until closing time. This is unless it's affected by sudden bad news, like a negative government announcement or a nasty fall on Wall Street. A tumbling Footsie won't help either.

I've found the biggest daily surge on a rising share price is frequently displayed on teletext at 11am. This may be because by now the big buyers have had a chance to settle themselves in their offices, do a bit of research into the share in question, and get confirmation for a purchase from their boss. As lunch-time nears, the share's ascent grinds to a halt. Sometimes it even decays slightly. It is lunch-time, after all. The next time a price change appears on your teletext screen is 3pm. Commonly, nothing much will have happened to your share since its last screen appearance at 1pm. Normal after-lunch doziness may be to blame for the slow-down.

Between 3pm and 4.30pm, investors seem to wake up again, and a share which is still in favour can make its biggest gain of the day. This is because would-be buyers, who've been optimistically waiting all day for a fall in the share price, now have very little time if they are to purchase stock on today's date. They fear that if they leave the transaction until tomorrow, overnight developments on foreign markets or a piece of early news at home could make the share even more expensive tomorrow.

All this suggests that a seller who wants to realise the best price for a rising share should resist doing anything most of the day, only calling his broker between 4pm and 4.30pm. While the buyer of a rising share should strike very early in the session to avoid the 11am surge.

The daily path of steadily rising stock can be reversed for a falling share, though the same sheep-like forces are at work. If an unlucky share begins the session down a few pence, it will often slide all day. It can slip most during the 'active zone' just before 11am. Then comes a moribund period when the share is flat. After 4pm the tumble starts again, as shareholders rush to sell before the day's end, fearing bigger falls tomorrow. This indicates that the buyer of a falling share should wait till the last minute. And a seller of sinking stock should act as soon as the market opens before matters get worse.

It's fair to warn you, though, that these daily timetables for a falling or rising share are extremely general. Don't bother to buy a stop-watch. Neither can they take into account the huge range of unforeseeable events which can unsettle individual firms or the market as a whole. And they don't allow for the effect of a single mind-blowing trade by a mammoth institutional seller or buyer.

Towards the end of the session, some sellers or buyers tend to panic. Remember that there is no law that says a share on a roll today will continue its rise tomorrow. Profit-takers are always ready to move in and reverse the action. While shares which have been plunging all day may easily start leaping tomorrow, when bargain hunters get cracking.

Weekly Pattern

If shares can rise and fall to a daily pattern, is there a similar model which can be applied to trading over a week? All things being equal, are some days better to sell or buy than others? Well, let's see. I've found that Monday sees a lot of market movement. This may be because investors have had two leisurely days in which to think and scheme. Though there's not much hard, corporate news over the weekend, there are bucket-loads of analysis and tips in the Sunday papers. Some punters can't wait to act upon it on Monday.

Yet the week's action sometimes gets off to a slow start, perhaps because desks tidied on Friday night take time to put into working order again. So if you want to take advantage of a Sunday journalist's tip, rise early and try to beat the rush. If you don't get through to your broker at first light, leave it a week or so when demand has petered out before you try again: the excitement of a newspaper tip soon burns out.

Thursdays, particularly the afternoons, can be quite lively. This is nothing special to the City. It's simply that slovenly types take until the fourth day to dispel the Monday morning feeling. You may have noticed that you get many more phone calls and mail on Thursdays. So if a share you fancy has been rising steadily earlier in the week, you might expect it to surge forward on Thursday. While a poorly share could well take a turn for the worse on that day.

The Friday Syndrome

Friday is a heavy day too, especially towards the close. Managers of the big institutions like to tidy up their books at the end of the week, so may be tempted to dispose of shares on Friday to start a clean sheet on Monday. Ordinary punters who've been dithering all week waiting for that favourable price which never came, will also take the plunge on Friday afternoon.

You'll know by now that it pays to be different and we should always buy when others sell. But there's another factor which should be considered before either buying or selling on a Friday – the Sunday Papers Effect. They contain financial stories which haven't come to light during the week because ambitious reporters have been sitting on them (people have more time to read their by-lines on Sundays). These may be good news stories, or they could be horrible shocks. And sub-editors, being what they are, are likely to give bigger headlines and more space to the negative reports. So on balance, Sunday paper reports – as opposed to tips – send shares in some companies down on Monday morning, making Friday a safer time to sell. However, the good news tales, which could concern thrilling take-over activity, will improve share prices when the Stock Exchange opens on Monday. So what to do? Well, if the company in question has been having a bad press lately, you might expect some more brickbats on Sunday. After all, where there's smoke, the hacks will find more smoke. But if positive stories abound on your company, perhaps another will hit the Sundays to send your share shooting north on Monday.

Small But Perfectly Formed

Why is a company like a balloon? Because it can go bang. Well, yes, but there's another answer. It's easier to make a small firm grow in size than it is to inflate a giant company which has already been puffed up nearly to its limits. A leading major in the Footsie develops only slowly, if at all, because it no longer has much growing room. Its share price may rise (or fall) in tune with the national economy, but its opportunities for breath-taking growth have gone AWOL. Smaller firms can rise further and faster because they still have a long way to go. Just a few orders can double their size just like that. Though you can imagine a small restaurant chain doubling its share price in six months, it's hardly likely that ICI could manage it. (Although it must be said that huge leviathans have the financial bulk to absorb unpleasant set-backs without causing a nasty crash. Small companies are not as well cushioned against such shocks.)

You'd be surprised how many huge conglomerates began life as tiddlers. And they are sometimes snapped up by giant squids. Which, if you are a shareholder in the small fry, is the best thing that could happen to you in the wonderful world of shares. Your holding will suddenly be very desirable – and you'll be squids in (sorry).

Some analysts prefer small companies because they often have a life of their own. They seem insulated against wild up-and-down

swings on the markets as a whole, particularly Wall Street. If New York plummets, followed by London, the shock blasts giant companies full on. But by the time the wave has reached humbler businesses, there may be no strength left in it – and they escape. Unfortunately, this means that a surge in market prices also likes to pass small firms by. But it's always better to avoid a loss than it is to make a profit, and the ability to escape both peaks and troughs of the Stock Exchange is easier on the nerves.

Penny Shares

Beginners think these are equities priced at one penny each. That's been known. But it simply means a cheap share, priced at less than 80p. They usually belong to companies which have skated on thin ice and haven't yet found a ladder to escape the pond. Some analysts scathingly refer to them as 'penny dreadfuls'.

They can indeed be perilous. I've invested in four penny shares companies which have disappeared without leaving as much as a footprint on that slender ice. Nobody even wrote to tell me the bad news, as there was no money left for stamps. However, for those who can afford to lose (and nobody should be dabbling in any kind of shares if they can't) they can be worth a fling. The rewards can be such that they will send you out to hire the Albert Hall for a party.

Supposing you buy shares in Browns Bottles for 2p each. If they now rise by a mere 2p you've doubled your money. If they're going to keep moving at all, it shouldn't be long before they hit 5p. And what if they then improve from 5p to 16p in a fortnight? I've known it happen. You invested £200. Now your shares are worth £1,600. Such an increase is hardly attainable by investing in a big company.

Ah yes, but what if your share falls? Well, if it staggers by as much as 50 per cent that's only a £100 loss. If it disappears altogether that's a £200 loss. Nasty, but you stood to gain £1,400 profit if all had gone well.

There is another enticing possibility with penny shares. Sometimes a firm which issues them is so strapped for cash to keep going that it announces a rights issue. This means you get a letter inviting you to buy even more shares (see the chapter A Rights Carry On). 'Not on your Nelly' did you say?

But hang on a minute. Organising a rights issue costs money. The directors realise their reputation is fragile at present. They don't want shareholders to turn down their proposal. So the new shares are offered at a thumping discount to the price you would pay on the stock market. True, the issue will probably dilute the current stock market price, but even so, you will still be able to buy the new shares cheaper. If the difference between issue and market price is just a halfpenny, because your shares are only worth 2p, you will do quite nicely, thank you.

But why should you risk it? After all, we know the company is tottering. Well, thrilling come-backs among small companies aren't that uncommon. There are several ways the directors can launch fast, remedial action. They can sell off subsidiary businesses, buildings and plant. They can bring in new management whiz kids to streamline operations. Or they could change the things they do or make.

Occasionally, beleaguered directors don't have to do anything much. What can happen – and it's a joyful day for ordinary investors when it does – is that a bold entrepreneur gallops to the rescue. He brings sacks of cash with him and swaps them for a managerial role and a stake in future profits.

Before he committed himself, our champion will have instructed his team to inspect the books – and you can bet he wouldn't risk his cash unless he thought there was life in the old firm yet. If you believe the new wonder boy is the type to take sensible precautions like this, you may be tempted to leave your funds in the company, even after the share price has risen to reflect the change in leadership. Though having said that, I have stayed loyal to penny share enterprises which were 'rescued' by an outsider, only to find the price has subsequently fallen back because the new broom failed to clean up a business which really was hopeless.

Cheap Shares

If a share is dirt cheap, 20p say, you might expect it to belong to a small company. But it doesn't always follow. The directors may have issued enough equities to fill a dozen warehouses. Totalled up, all those 20ps give the company a hefty value. So if you intend to invest in a small venture, hoping it will grow faster than a medium-sized or large company, then don't use the share price as a guide to size. Look up the value of the firm (market capitalisation) in your newspaper. It's the third column from the right in the *Financial Times*. Anything under a few million pounds is a very small company by Stock Exchange standards.

As a firm expands, its shares become dearer, making them harder to sell. So now and then, a company will halve the value of its equities at a stroke. But this isn't as drastic a move as it seems. So that armies of heavily-armed investors don't storm the glass doors at the company HQ, everyone's shareholding is doubled at the same time. So they are now, in theory, no better or worse off. Directors usually explain to investors on the register that the operation will make their shares 'easier to trade'. The real reason is to suck in more punters by making the stock seem more of a bargain. We all like to get more for our money and that goes for shares, even if these particular shares are worth half what they used to be.

But nobody should mind if this manoeuvre – it's called a one for one scrip issue, by the way – takes place. Having bags of shares in a company has an advantage over holding a few, even if the total value is the same. Here's an example. Jo has 5,000 shares in Amalgamated Teapots at 10p each. Robin has 500 shares in The Saucer Corporation at £1 each. Both have spent £500 in companies in the same sector of the market. Each firm has a similar track record and the same scintillating prospects for the future. Both enterprises are worth the same, but Amalgamated Teapots has ten times as many shares at large.

Equities in The Saucer Corporation rise by 20p one day. Amalgamated Teapots notch up only a 5p improvement. At first blush, Robin thinks he's profited more with The Saucer Corp. than Jo has with Amalgamated Teapots. But not so. Jo's shares may have only risen by 4p, but she has 5,000 of them, giving her the bigger gain of £200. Robin's 500 shares rose by an impressive 20p each, but he only makes £100.

Logically, if both companies make exactly the same progress, every time Amalgamated Teapots' price goes up by 1p, The Saucer Corporation's equities should leap by 10p. But in reality this difference is unlikely to be maintained and Jo's holding in Amalgamated Teapots will make the most money. This case illustrates one of the best arguments for investing in penny shares: you get an enormous number of shares for a modest outlay, helping investors to benefit by the above anomaly.

Dozing Pennies

Sometimes penny shares languish for years with no improvement in profits nor any fresh injections of capital. But patience may come in handy here. You might expect cheap shares to jump up and down ferociously, because the company's not solid enough to bestow any gravity. But 'pennies' are often the most stationary of all stocks. So once you've invested, it's possible to view them as a sleeper to tuck away in a bottom drawer. Sometimes, perhaps when a handsome prince, in the shape of an ambitious new chief executive, comes along to give the kiss of life, penny sleepers spring to life and start to party. As I write, a health care company has risen from 4p to 17p in a few weeks, after being stuck around the lower figure for over a year.

However, it must be acknowledged that some penny share companies eventually vanish from the listings. And with shares priced so low they haven't very far to fall before a crash, so you haven't much time to see the ground rushing up before using the ejector seat.

Some ways to Spot a Winning Tiddler

Plans to invest in a small company call for more care than a giant enterprise which will already have been researched by analysts with the big institutions. The price set for a big company share is therefore more likely to be 'fair' than a smaller company. With a bantam firm you are often on your own. Don't rush into buying shares; first try to discover all you can about it. It would be sensible to send for the last annual report and try to make sense of the figures. You should also study any snippets in the papers. Of course, humbler firms don't attract lots of publicity and you may have to wait some time before you know enough about the company to buy with confidence. The wait is worth it. During a bull run, for example, it's been found that equities in smallish firms do consistently better than big ones.

Special Shares

In a fair world, shares in companies would steadfastly ascend if their earnings improved year after year. But some lucky firms attract more investment than their profit-and-loss accounts deserve, because of the sort of things they make or services they provide. These fortunates may be worth investing in because of their 'hidden assets'. As we'll see, some of their attractions wouldn't be at all alluring if we lived in a sane world.

Boring, Boring, Boring

Where there's muck there's brass, and companies which make grommets, tappets, bearings and plastic coatings stand as much, if not more chance of making dosh as any other business. But because of their boring, grey, grimy image, the share price isn't always as strong as the company deserves. No point in investing in them, then. But wait! Private investors may be put off by a dingy image, but the hard-headed managers of pension funds and insurance companies aren't swayed by such things.

The institutions are often compelled to ignore small companies, because they can't buy enough stock, but minnows grow into bigger fish. And when they do, analysts working for the really big spenders will quickly pounce on the shares if they're selling at bargain prices, whether the product is ho-hum or breathtakingly exciting. So if you invest in a small engineering business with an uninteresting product, you may be glad you did in a few years' time. To satisfy yourself that the shares of such a company really are cheap you could look at the PE (Price to Earnings) ratio in the *Financial Times*. If it's a lower figure than that showing for similar outfits, take it as a good sign.

Glamour Shares

We investors can be a starry-eyed lot. This means that companies operating in a glamorous, glitzy, show biz world can attract more investment than their money-making prowess merits. These include TV companies, film makers and fashion houses. Some punters entertain fantasies of their holding doing so well that

they're eventually invited on to the board, from which lofty postion they can lord it over big stars. Pure bunkum, and they know it, but even an impossible dream makes 'glamour shares' attractive to some people.

To a secondary extent, some investors are strangely attracted to national newspapers, breweries, toy makers, airlines and holiday tour operators. Perhaps they secretly hope for free samples.

All this silliness can help to make 'glamour shares' overbought and dear. But that may not be a good reason to stand aside. Some investors find it such a nice thought to own a piece of show business that they find it very hard to let go, come what may. This helps to shove up the share price and curb general market set-backs.

A related reason why glamour shares are wont to ride high is that some star-struck captains of industry forever lust after prominent positions of power. Have you ever read of a shortage of prospective buyers for a national newspaper? Others can't wait to get hands on a TV company, producing a few bids and even more rumours. But before staying with, or buying into a 'glamorous' company, once again check the PE rating. If it's a higher figure than other companies in the same stable, then, if there are no extra advantages in sight, the price might be too high – even for a piece of show biz.

Shares With A Kick

Talking about glamorous shares, we've all noticed the burgeoning number of soccer clubs 'going public'. And whatever the clubs' fortunes, there will be many more to come. As well as attracting ordinary investors, soccer shares appeal to fans who regard them as souvenirs. Some brokers even offer to frame football share certificates which are bought through them. The shares are also occasionally snapped up by business moguls and celebrities who can afford to buy their way on to the board. Football fans who are not particularly loyal to the club in question chip in for shares simply because they like to support their number one game. Money flows in and the share price rises, even if turnstile takings, together with income from replica kits and other spin-offs, don't merit the interest. There's also the certainty that an ever-increasing number of TV stations will pay obscene sums to screen the top clubs in action.

Soccer clubs have a special advantage. Most companies listed on the Stock Exchange don't have forgiving shareholders whose backing can be relied upon whatever the scale of imminent disaster. As clubs are at least partly insulated by loyalty from the cruel forces which upset the markets, it may be worth booting a team into your portfolio, even if you can't stand the game.

But, as soccer is a funny old game, what if your chosen club goes bust? Well, it's not likely. All a struggling club has to do is issue more shares, and fans, mortified by the prospect of oblivion for their team, will cheerfully cough up. Either that or a millionaire pop star or proprietor of a retail chain will materialise with a bulging wallet.

There's another thing going for soccer shares – they appeal to hopeless share addicts like me. Once the Stock Exchange reaches close of play on Friday, there's nothing to get the old juices going at the weekend – except football results. For the owner of football shares, that delicious market tension continues over Saturday and Sunday. If Tottenham Hotspur lose, Monday's price will be subdued. If Manchester United blast enough leather into the rigging (see, I even write like a sports hack) the shares will rise.

When a club forces its way to join the top few in its league, the excitement intensifies. Each goal they score carries investors nearer to a strapping share rise. Every disappointment makes the prospect of losing money more real. New signings, real or speculative, also tweak share prices, as do changes of manager or a new TV deal.

But which clubs are most likely to realise your investment goals? Well, you need to look at the form. Teams go in and out of form. Their runs of success or failure last for several weeks, or months. The lads may be playing 'blinders', at the peak of their careers. Or they may be ravaged by colds, flu, back strains, cartilage problems, stiff necks, debt, messy scandals, domestic dramas, murder charges and so on.

In soccer, once a losing streak is underway it's hard to shrug off. A loss of confidence is a growing beast. Even when a team is on form, it's hard to stay on top, because the teams up there with you are enjoying equally heady times. If your team loses for four or five weeks on the trot, you might care to boot your money into touch until better times. Hopeless optimism is for real fans, only.

Fancy Names

There are punters who bet on a racehorse because they like its name. More surprisingly, there are folk who invest in a company for the sole reason that its title rather tickles them. An imaginative name for an enterprise might take their fancy because it's comic, down-to-earth, picturesque, exotic or all four. Toad, Tadpole, Sycamore, Sleepy Kids are examples. I'm not recommending or advising against any of these particular enterprises. But in share listings and newspaper headlines, their odd names do stare at us from the print. Unlike names like Amalgamated Holdings or Galvanised Zinc. Does the mere name of a company pull in more investors? Probably. One reason why the board of a new company chooses a wacky name is to bring it to the notice of customers, and make it hard to forget thereafter. They're also trying to attract the attention of stock-pickers who may be loath to invest in something they have never heard of. A peculiarity of a quirky name is that it sounds very familiar. You may think that having a conspicuous name is a senseless reason to pump money into a venture – but if it is happening, you might consider taking advantage of the rising share price. To invest in a funny name is a daft idea, but to invest because others invest because it is a funny name, is a different matter.

Also, an imaginative humorous name might also reveal an imaginative board of directors with a sense of humour. Whether or not you take this as a signal to buy the shares depends if you equate a sense of fun with intelligence and ambition. I do. However, don't take these arguments as a strong inducement to invest in a firm with a queer name and no other selling points. An out-of-the-ordinary title is a rather trivial indicator. As always, you should look at a whole basket of pointers before taking the plunge.

Tele-Shares

Some shares appear on the two main teletext services because they
are big players. But the ITV service will put more modest companies up there in lights – if they pay for the privilege like their
bigger brothers do. All the investors I know watch both the ITV
and BBC services, so the names of fairly small companies are thrust
before their faces daily. This makes some more modest ventures
pretty well known. The intention of paying to put your company
on the screen is to attract more investment and hopefully improve
share prices. Daily reminders might also attract more customers for
the company's goods or services, which should also bolster the
price. It's therefore possible that these shares are over-priced. Or
the daily exposure might actually bring in new orders and provide
money for expansion, in which case they could be bargains. If the
progress of a minor company on teletext steadily rises you might
take this as a healthy sign. But if you want to know if the share has
become over-bought, you can either check for a low price-to-earnings ratio (PE) in the financial pages or ask your broker.

Seizing the Moment

Even in its quietest periods there is always something happening in the stock market. Scandals, mergers, take-over bids (real or rumoured) and new flotations are ready to break up the tedium when shares are neither rising nor falling. And a nimble-witted investor can profit from almost any of these situations – if she jumps the right way. Here are some typical market 'stories' with advice on how you may be able to exploit them.

The Dragging Take-Over

Some people like hearing bells on Sunday, the Moonlight Sonata, or champagne fizzing. But for sheer joy, you can't beat the whisper of a take-over rumour – if you own a slice of the company in the alleged firing line. Daily price rises will be dramatic while the fun lasts. If you don't own some of the lucky stock, it may be worth looking at the firm which is surmised to be the 'target', even if you personally think this particular bid speculation is a load of old toffee. But you need to act quickly. The action can be short-lived, especially if the supposed raider spoils the fun by making a statement denying everything.

If no such announcement is made the rise may still peter out when nothing appears to be happening. Such a state of uncertainty can loiter around for years. During this limbo, the price will rise and fall as confidence in the vaunted take-over swells or wanes. A typical pattern might be that on the rumour's first day or two, the share betters itself by around 50p. Then it begins to shed a few pence daily for two weeks as the doubters systematically jump ship. The share now begins a period of stagnation, perhaps lasting some months. Suddenly, on a renewed murmur, it takes off again, soon to recover all lost ground. Then silence returns and the share begins another stately descent . . .

Nimble investors can 'get a result' more than once out of take-over rumours even if the story is far-fetched and never happens. One strategy is to buy at first hint of a bid and sell when the climb runs out of steam. Buy when it bottoms out and wait for the rumour to revive and heave the price upwards again. Easier said than done, of course. But if the take-over rumours continue on and off for a lengthy period it may be possible to work out a pattern to act on. As many other investors will be playing the same game, you need to try and act a little earlier each time than your fancy might otherwise dictate.

Old hands say you need an iron will to play this game. They know it's difficult to sell and take profits after a big leap in case there's more ice-cream in the tub. They force themselves. It's also hard to buy shares back after a series of falls, because it's human nature to expect worse to come. Remember, too, that the 'shall I, shan't I' judgements you will need to make are so delicately poised that it's easy to miss out on big rewards. This game could be called Musical Shares. One day the music might stop, the take-over will be confirmed, and you could be left without any newly-expensive shares to sit on.

If the vast majority of rumour stories did come true, then it would be best to sit tight until the happy day when a marriage date is set. But as you come to realise many rumours never mature, the in-and-out strategy does become more engaging.

There are handy ways of assessing if a take-over story might be genuine. To begin with, you can get a good idea by hints in the press and minor manoeuvring by the firms involved. If you hear a quote from a chief executive which sounds very much like a denial that a take-over is on the cards, read the words carefully again. 'We're concerned about unfounded speculation in the City...' is not a denial, though it's clearly meant to be. Neither is: 'A take-over is not envisaged at present.' Well no, but it might happen in the future – say two weeks' time. You might also learn that the possible predator already has a large stake in the possible target. Was this built up with take-over in mind? Probably. Does the target company own lots of land, buildings, plant and other stuff that a plundering company would like to get its mitts on? Do you think the target has a lower share price than it ought to have? These are all possible signs that a bid is on the horizon.

The Vague Plague

The City hums with take-over rumours all the time. Many of these yarns have no basis in fact, but they spread unchecked because of the ever-present greed factor. The fairy tale soon speeds beyond City boundaries so that relatives, friends and neighbours ring you up to tell you 'the good news'. City sages shake heads over gin and tonics and mumble the old adage 'You should never buy on a rumour.' But some shares, which are the centrepiece of a take-over story, often adopt a pattern which a nippy investor may be able to milk profitably. Fancy an example?

Fly-by-night Airlines Ltd are scorned by the market. The shares have languished at 2p for years. Some mischievous soul invents a 'possible take-over' for them and they rise a penny. This is a massive 50 per cent hike which nevertheless goes unnoticed – though it would cause a sensation if it happened to a mammoth like ICI. Eagle-eyed investors spot the flurry in the *Financial Times* share listings and, though they haven't heard the rumour, perceive something is happening. They throw money in – and the shares are marked up to 4p. More investors become excited and the price mounts to 5p. This represents a mouth-watering return for the lucky ones who paid 2p, so they cash in their chips. The price now dips to 3p. People who thought they'd missed the bus and balked at paying 5p, plus the broker's cut, suddenly hear the vehicle coming round the block again and leap on board. The price breaks more ground, rising to 6p. But the supposed take-over never happens – and the price gradually returns to its customary resting place of 2p.

This common sequence of 'up, down, up further and down for good' often happens in the case of penny shares which are subject to unfounded rumour. Full-time investors are uneasy with any strategy based on the nebulous. But if you think you see a pattern emerging, it's possible to take advantage, even though you are damn sure the bid talk is pure bunkum. But you need to be nippy, as it can be all over in a few weeks.

As you get a lot of shares for your outlay the stake can be quite small, though as with all penny shares, the wide spread and dealing costs take their toll.

You may want to know if there is a way of protecting yourself from coming out of the investment too soon if, by some fluke, the vague rumour of a bid turns out to be true. One gambit would be to buy when the share has risen on two consecutive days. Ride the share until the first fall, then sell half. Now wait for momentum to gather again – and sell the rest when the share price just beats its earlier high. Fine if it happens. But of course the first fall may be the last and the second rise might not materialise. So please don't blame me.

Do Shells Suit?

You come across a small listed company without much capital which seems to be doing very little. It's not gobbling up any other firms or acquiring assets and the profits are either becalmed or falling. This could be worth looking into. The firm may be a 'shell' waiting to happen. Energetic entrepreneurs are always searching for shells. You invest a packet in them and suddenly you're in charge of an outfit quoted on the Stock Exchange. This is a lot less trouble and costly than forming and floating a listed company yourself. You can either build on the firm's usual activities or sell its plant and buildings to navigate it into quite different waters.

For share-pickers, the ideal situation is to invest in the host company before the invasion (though usually it's more of an invitation). Sometimes the rebirth of a shell takes a maddening long time, but the rewards can be beefy enough to revitalise any flagging portfolio. Some of the best shell prospects have had nasty problems in the recent past, so their shares are pretty cheap. This gives the private investor the chance to buy an awful lot of equities for a modest outlay. When the chap on the shining white horse arrives, each share should rise by a tidy amount. And as you've got armfuls the rewards will be yummy.

But even though you've now got a valuable investment in the company it may not be right for you to sell your shares straight away. If somebody has taken the risk of injecting money into a lowly company, he must have enthusiastic plans for it. It may be worth hanging on to his coat-tails for a while. After all, you could always sell if the share price starts to retreat again.

So far, all I've said about exploiting possible shells makes the process seem hunky-dory. But there are snags. You may wait a long time for Mr Right to come along. Four or five years isn't so unusual.

During the fallow period, dividends aren't likely and your money will be denied bank interest. The share price may dwindle further during the long wait. And that could turn into a long goodbye if a rescuer doesn't come at all. You may have to cut your losses by scrambling out. There is always a chance that the shares may spark into a new life on their own, if trading conditions improve, perhaps, or a new managing director is brought in. But if nothing happens you may be in trouble.

The risk is cut, though, if you pick a shell company with the right attractions for an entrepreneur and his money. I asked some of my City sources for a few pointers. Most importantly, a shell needs to have a low capitalisation (not worth much). Then find out if a sizeable amount of its share issue already belongs to another company. If so, the other firm might be interested in taking over the management. Finally, if you think you've found a company which qualifies as a shell be prepared to wait years after you've invested for something to happen.

Suspended Shares

Look out for companies which are suspended on the Stock Exchange. Some shares can no longer be traded for the time being because of a price sensitive development, like a merger. But share-pickers need only be concerned with those firms which are suspended because something has gone wrong. This could be a major mistake in the accounts, managerial incompetence, fraud, sharply falling share values or some other kind of corporate catastrophe.

Often these suspensions stay in force for quite some time. But keep a watch for their return. By the time normal trading resumes, the problems of the company in question should have been fully sorted out. Even so, the share price will probably topple from its price immediately before the suspension, often to a very low level. This is because nervous investors didn't have time to sever connections before the suspension and are falling over themselves to get out now. With so many jumping ship, the new price of the share soon slips to far less than it's worth.

One strategy here is to wait for the share to stabilise – it may still fall even further – then buy. Once a share like this starts moving upwards, its progress can be rapid. But I have seen a 600 per cent profit almost wiped out shortly afterwards, because I've been too greedy. At the very first whiff of a rocket failure, take profits fast. True, the ride may continue upwards for a while, but it's more likely that the rising share is being powered by quick profiteers like yourself and is thus defying gravity. Only rarely does a previously suspended share make a fast comeback to the heady values it enjoyed before suspension.

Exploiting Company Crashes

Some high-flying investors, vulture-like, relish the crash of a large firm. They're aware that its customers will have to go somewhere else. So they hurriedly pump money into one or more of the ill-fated company's more obvious rivals. The fewer firms there are in the field of operation, the more beneficial they expect their specu-lation to be. The thinking seems sound enough. If a firm making electrical potato-peelers crashes, shares in the only other firm making them are surely going to rise. But hang on! Suppose the collapse happened because the public no longer wants electric potato peelers at any price. Then the competitive firms will also sink from sight.

What the sensible investor does in this situation is to inspect the product or service on offer and ask if she needs it herself or knows lots of people who might. Is what is on offer a fad or something which has an exhilarating future?

Brash Upstarts

You know the story. A new company is born with a blaring fanfare in the press and a snappy advertising slogan which pops up on TV, radio, and on poster hoardings everywhere. To make such waves of publicity, the newcomer doubtless has colossal backing from big City players. But what if the firm is marching, with trumpets sounding, on to a battlefield which is already well-popu-lated by competitors? Well, if you rate those rivals you might think twice about falling for all that hype. Take phone companies for instance. When a new one, bristling with cash from presti-gious backers, comes into being it takes its chance with all the other providers. True, the new company may have cheaper, better technology than its rivals. But has it? Perhaps you shouldn't go ahead till you've found out. A delay will also give the ballyhoo and puffery a chance to settle down. And if you're unsure even when the heat has died down, you might still prefer to stay out of the kitchen.

A Clear Direction

You're listening to the morning's business slot on Radio Four. Something exciting is happening to a firm you've had your eye on for some time. It may be bidding for a rival, defending a take-over, laying off workers, or opening a new plant. Any one of these developments could massage the share price – or topple it. Unless you're an insider on top of the company's plans, it's hard to predict how the market will react. How many times, for instance, have you heard bumper profits announced on the news, only to see, when you tune into a teletext service, that the share has actually fallen? The reason is because influential brokers have previously publicised their predictions that the company in question will post large profits. Their forecasts have already been factored into the share price. However, the actual margins came in at the lower end of high expectations. So although hefty profits were eventually announced, they weren't hefty enough. The market frowned and the share price fell. The lesson to be drawn from this everyday tale can be found in the old City maxim: 'Never mind the news, feel the direction.' In other words, wait to see if the share takes an upward or downward direction, after reporting its annual or half-year results, before taking any action.

Exactly how you should proceed is still a question, though. If the share falls, you might look for another haven for your money. Or if you think the reasoning behind the fall is suspect, you might go 'bargain hunting' once the share has reached its new lowly level. If the share soars, however, you could either jump on board expecting the price to rise even more, or take a view that the share is becoming over-valued and steer clear. But don't do anything until you have first identified the 'direction'.

New, Are We?

Should you invest in that new technology firm which has just been floated? After all, you like the cut of its jib, and it seems a spiffing idea to jump in there first. Wait a minute, though. Start-up costs often prevent new concerns from making profits in the first few years. By the time it really gets going, the fledgeling company's market could have changed. Their computers may no longer be wanted. If the venture succeeds, an early bird who puts his money up before the big shekels start rolling in, will get more worms. Even so, an experienced investor is more likely to wait until he knows which way the wind blows. He reckons that the day when a young company first emerges, blinking, into the daylight of profitability is the best time to latch on. By then the heart-stopping uncertainty will be over and the new-comer may soon change into that marvellous thing – a slow steady riser.

Annual Reports

Every year, a company makes a full report on its progress over 12 months. Between times it makes an interim summary so that shareholders get a picture of progress or lack of it every six months. Annoyingly, we don't get a copy of either document through the post until a while after it's first published. So big institutions, always deemed by the City to be more important than general punters, have the first chance to act on the information. True, the edited highlights of an annual or half-time report will often be reported by the press. But City professionals will still know the details before you and me.

But a newspaper story based on an annual report is still useful. If the writer suggests, after sifting through its pages, that the reporting company is doing much better than it was, that should encourage a rush by readers to buy shares. But many private investors, pedantic to the core, don't believe anything in the papers. They wait for the report's arrival on the doormat so they can check the balance sheet personally. If they're pleased with what they see, they may buy more shares. So once copies of the company report arrive in Acacia Avenue, the price often rises again. The advice then is act soon after a favourable write-up and before you receive the annual report through your letterbox. Against popular belief, newspaper summaries are rarely wrong. And just as helpfully, financial journalists are trained to read between the lines and sort wheat from chaff. You may not beat the institutions in the race to buy, but you could steal a march on fellow private investors. You will also save yourself the eye-aching chore of sifting through the small print and figures, most of which only accountants can distinguish from double Dutch.

On the other hand, if journalists tell you that your company has failed to impress them, you could dispose of your shares, rather than wait for the company report's arrival. Heavy selling might well begin again, once the public get hold of the fine details. If, on finally receiving your fat envelope, with its second class stamp, you scan finer details in the report and begin to regret selling, you can always buy in again. Should the price have fallen further in the meantime, you will get more shares for your money.

Another tip on annual and half-time reports is to note down the date they come out. This helps next year. As a company nears its reporting day, the price can start trundling upwards. This is because well-known brokers have already estimated profits. If you don't know when the figures will be published, you may miss this opportunity. Conversely, the share price may tumble a daily penny or two in the week before the report comes out. In this case you may want to pull out before the grim day.

Reading Annual Reports

Some worthy guides on share dealing urge you to study a company's annual report in detail. A gushing chairman's report is thought to be an especially good omen. But take off your rose-tinted glasses first. The board of directors use this document to put themselves in the best possible light. Maybe it's no coincidence that the chairman's report comes at the beginning. After a lousy year, he can easily concoct what appears to be a magnificent success story by leaving out the nasty bits. He knows some shareholders never get beyond the first few pages to study figures towards the back which may cast a different light. And as for the section of the chairman's report which looks to the future, well, he could say anything.

Wily investors keep their old annual reports in sock drawers so they can compare them with the latest issue. It may be as thick and glossy as earlier productions, but does it carry as much hard news? Are there lots of photos of smiling directors and apparently enthusiastic workers, where last year there were plentiful facts about developing sales and assets? If so there may be something nasty in the woodshed which they're trying to hide.

The annual report will display all the figures. But as they give a picture how things stand on one day only, the accounts will be totally out of date when you get them. A public company's records can legally be up to six months behind the times when they're presented to shareholders.

There are plenty of other snags about annual or half-yearly accounts. Sometimes a dazzling profit is shown when the money hasn't actually come into company coffers yet. In fact, it may never arrive and that 'profit' could really be a loss which threatens the company's very existence. Despite efforts to stamp it out, creative accountancy can do lots of things with company balances to make the garden seem rosier than it is. Sadly you need heavy qualifications, and probably a lot more information, to see through all the smoke-screens.

Classy Reports

There are some interesting clues about a company to be gleaned from its annual report. Mouldy Cheese Products Ltd is a small listed concern with profits bordering on losses and weighty debts. Yet it produces a thick, shiny report with fancy artwork. Does it have directors who tend towards lobbing money at drains? It would seem like it. The chairman will no doubt argue that the annual report has to be impressive because it acts as a 'calling card'. It has to encourage potential customers and more investment from shareholders.

But for all its luxury, the Mouldy Cheese Products Ltd report still manages to be old-fashioned and poorly written. The prose in statements from the chairman and his executives is deadly dull, heavy with vague jargon, and couched in eccentric grammar. Nobody's saying you should junk one of your favourite firms just because its principals have made a mess of the annual report, but there's no harm in taking the fact into consideration with all other indicators.

What about the annual report of a leading company, a high street bank, say? In this case the document can be as expensive as they like: it's a drop in an ocean of resources. But the style could still appear old-fashioned, stodgy and pompous. This could be a hint the bank is trailing the times. Read between the lines. Is there too little mention of new technologies, initiatives and ideas? This could flag a loss of pace in today's fiendishly-competitive banking rat race. There may be more progressive institutions which deserve your share money.

Vital Statistics

Many annual reports include photographs of board members. Top investors would never admit it, as it seems unscientific, but they do peer at these pictures closely. Do the directors look like thrusting types, bursting with aspiration, ambition and drive? Or do they come across as smug, apathetic, or lazy? Do their modes of dress make it look as if they mugged a tramp on their way to the office? In Shakespeare's play, *Julius Caesar*, that early corporate raider says he would rather have round him people who are fat. He's worried about a chap called Cassius who has a 'lean and hungry look'. He's right not to trust Cassius, a politician so fired by ambition that he masterminds a plan to do Caesar in. So if you want a ruthlessly ambitious board of directors to send your shares roaring away, perhaps you should search annual reports for pictures of lean, hungry-looking directors, preferably in togas, with special attention to managing directors, chairmen and chief executives.

It should be said that not all my informants agree that slender directors are necessarily the most dynamic. That trim, sprightly figure may be the result of wasting too much time on the golf course or squash courts. And there's a possibility that slim directors are so worried about future prospects that they're shedding pounds under the stress. And remember that if an executive is overweight it doesn't necessarily mean he's complacent. The poor bloke may have had a generous figure forced on him by too many champagne lunches at which he's successfully negotiated some bumper deals.

If there are close-up portraits in the report you can find more clues to character in a director's face than in his general appearance. Does it have grim lines of determination and piercing eyes, or does he look rather bemused or even a bit dopey?

But don't be put off by directors who, in their dress and hairstyle, look like nerds. We all know that people at the pinnacle of technical know-how, top number-crunchers and accountancy wizards often do have this appearance. Having a few of these types on the board of a company is an encouraging sign.

Who's on Board?

Another thing to check for in the group photo of the board is if there are women present. This is the mark of a company which, by valuing sexual equality, displays a modern outlook. The higher up women are in the pecking order, the more enlightened you can expect the firm to be. Of course women will occupy boardroom chairs in fashion houses, interior design groups, and the like, but it's when they have authority in heavier spheres – like engineering and transport – that their presence becomes significant.

One of the darker habits of professional investors is to study how many directors are getting on in years. They may soon need to be replaced. This could be a good or bad thing, depending on the veteran's track record. An experienced war horse may have trampled down the competition over the years. His successor may lack the same entrepreneurial spirit. Another possibility, though, is that the old boy may have been a business ace once, but has now lost his

MANAGING DIRECTOR

touch. You can't make any significant guesses about this by putting a company photo under a magnifying glass, but you may get an indication by studying the sharpness of his written report. You could also look out for any profiles of him in the newspapers. If you think the top dog has lost his bite you might want to put your money somewhere else.

However, it's a different kettle of fish if most of the board is on the elderly side. Directors who are winding down often court the attention of other firms which are on the take-over trail. They may commend a merger to shareholders as good commercial sense, but they also know that such a deal will feather their retirement nests. So if you have a holding in a company with an exceptionally elderly board, it might be worth hanging on to your shares in case a bidder comes along. A take-over is usually the best thing that can happen to a share price.

The Attitude

If you don't make an uncommonly high number of mistakes, investing in shares will usually come right in the end. Most companies build up their profits year after year. Being a shareholder means you own a part of those enterprises, so you should do all right. You won't get very far if you scatter your investment money around with a blunderbuss, though. Share-picking calls for some pretty fine judgements in situations which are always changing. Investment is all about that most difficult of human activities – making decisions. But there are only two choices really – when to buy and when to sell.

Some wise soul once told me that if you really can't decide between two options, then it doesn't matter which way you go, because both stand an equal chance of being right. This may apply in real life, but not to the stock market. Decisions here are always hard but if you make the wrong choice it costs you a lot of bus fares. This book is full of hints on which way to jump, but as no-one really knows the future, you are, I'm afraid, on your own. However considered your investment choices have been, if you have ill-luck, it can all go wrong. Here are some hints to help you cope with the uncertainty of it all.

The Right Frame of Mind

You are handicapped in the share game if you haven't got, or aren't willing to acquire, the 'right attitude'. You must not be so fearful about your speculations that you lie awake at night. One way to avoid worrying, as told to me by a fund manager who trades in millions, is to forget about a deal the second you put the phone down. If you can keep the transaction out of your mind for a full three minutes, you probably won't be plagued by 'Good-grief-what-have-I-done' thoughts several times a day. Should you allow yourself to have a panic about your trade in the first few minutes after making it, niggling worries will hang around for months.

The Big Controller

The most famous investors in the world get it wrong sometimes, probably a lot more than they let on. Admitting your judgement has been faulty is a hard thing to do – especially to yourself. Because of this human frailty, we tend to stay with some very duff shares, come what may. We search for reasons to keep them while ignoring mountains of evidence to the contrary. If we can't find justification for retaining our white elephants, we hang on anyway.

City professionals have even more pride in their share-picking than amateurs. But they're not so vulnerable to its pitfalls. Their superiors insist on fixed 'stop loss' limits. If a share does badly, its kicked out of a big institution's portfolio. There's positively no argument about it. That's one reason why a share can pitch a long way down following a small blip. The share collides with a big investor's stop limit. Heavy selling duly takes place. As a result, the price drops further and argues with another fund manager's cut-off price further down the scale. And so the heart-stopping fall continues. Until, that is bargain hunters start sniffing around the ill-starred share and send it skywards again.

But an individual investor is in a different boat. She has no superior being in the form of a cautious boss, to insist that enough is enough and that her stop limits positively must be adhered to. Without an outside discipline, she may fail to cut her losses because she simply can't admit defeat.

To be a top-flight investor, you need all the skills of the calling, not just the talent to pick good shares. One of those vital attributes is self-control. You have to constantly psyche yourself up to stamp out those profit-destroying emotions of self-regard and arrogance.

Pride And Prejudice

When you're sowing mistakes, there's no more fertile ground than the stock market. It has to be faced – you're going to make lots of blunders. Don't be down-hearted though. As somebody once said, 'If you get it 55 per cent right then you're doing better than most of the professionals.' It's fairly important you realise this because a false feeling of infallibility can force you into hot water. The earlier you accept you made a bloomer by plumping for the wrong share, the sooner you can act to correct it. Don't allow false pride to tell you a failure is a success in disguise. While you're hamstrung by this thought, a rogue share has extra time to plunge further. Pride is the devilish spur which makes you kid yourself that a hopeless share is 'going to come right in the end'. Never say this – unless you have very tough evidence that you are right.

One reason that City analysts use computers nowadays is to quash interference from human emotions. Machines haven't got any pride. Their 'decisions' to buy or sell are based on hard data, not a protection against hurt feelings. Though having said that, most sensible share researchers will always add their own judgement to the pot before making a 'buy' or 'sell' suggestion. Why do human share-pickers have advantages over computers? If you put all the known information about a company into a computer and ask it if you should buy shares in it, you'll get an answer. But it will never be a complete answer. It doesn't matter how well a machine is programmed, it will also always be short of some of the thousands of tiny scraps of information we humans collect from the ether and subconsciously use to make our hunches.

Getting Cocky?

Had a string of early successes, have you? Been telling everybody that 'doing shares' is a licence to make brass? Feel you can't go wrong? I'm happy for you – except that this sounds like beginner's luck which could lead to disaster. Confidence is a useful share-picker's tool – when tempered with caution. Over-confidence is fatal.

Being too cocksure overtakes most investors sooner rather than later. It happened to me when I first put a toe in the quicksands of 'traded equity' options. This is a risky off-shoot of the share realm which calls for razor-sharp judgement and strict self-discipline. Just the sort of qualities which are marred by over-confidence. This is my sad story.

I bought British Gas options for £500. Shortly afterwards, there were rumours of a take-over bid by Shell. I was able to sell my options and made £2,000 profit in a few months. Other successes followed in fast succession with share options in the British Airports Authority and British Telecom. I was doing too well, too fast. By now feeling that I had entered a gold mine, I quickly bought options in seven other companies, doing hardly any home-work on any of them. Disaster! Two of these hasty selections soon published dire warnings about their future profits. These grim forecasts immediately depressed two of my other chosen com-panies. Both events collided with a bad mood in the markets and my other three options also failed to meet their target prices. So all seven options had to be abandoned at a total loss.

It took me 10 years of ordinary share trading before I entered the traded option arena because I knew it to be dead risky. But I threw away a lot of money in a few weeks because over-confidence crowded all that useful experience of market behaviour from my brain. Fortunately, I've never had to tussle with over-confidence in my ordinary share dealings, because I didn't do at all well in my first year. But if you have some big successes early in a share-picking career you almost certainly face the risk.

When I ask experienced share traders how to curb over-confi-dence, one tip they give is tot up all your gains and losses to find the balance at least every two months. If you're beginning to think you are king of the castle, this little exercise should bring you down to earth with a bump. Your audit will probably show your share performance isn't as stunning as you thought. This is because we're all rather good at revelling in our winners while conveniently disregarding the lemons. You may have noticed the syndrome while checking daily share prices in the paper. You mentally cheer when one of your shares sidles upwards by 5p while shrugging off a 15p drop in another of your selections. Most share-pickers are cock-eyed optimists – it's what attracts them to the markets in the first place.

Bragging

Boasting is easy to recognise in others, hard to spot in yourself. You think you're harmlessly discussing shares with friends. But you keep mentioning your winners, never your failures. This is bad manners. Someone in the group may have sold the same successful shares before they took off. You'll make her feel terrible and yourself unpopular. Switch the emphasis to your downfalls. Your friends will have an opportunity to learn from your mistakes. They may also save you money – by making helpful comments about your strategy which you haven't even thought about.

Strategies

There are some who frown on the concept of a 'system' when used in relation to share investment. It smacks too much of gambling. Racing fans and roulette players use systems. Analysts and other posh people in the City use strategies. Here then are a few investment strategies which have proved to be heartily robust so far – though of course nobody can speak for the future.

The Longest Play

This investment policy dates back a long way. It was used by the famous economics genius, John Maynard Keynes, in the thirties. It's followed by many, but its ideal adherent is Job, because you need serious patience. It's very basic: you buy shares in a few leading companies and don't do anything else, leaving them to appreciate in value over many years. You take no notice of market fluctuations and you certainly don't dip in and out in pursuit of fast, if modest profits. Records show that this system is as sound as any you're likely to come across. You also need to be a miser, because you won't get a chance to spend your profits unless you interfere with the system by selling your holding. Even the dividends should be re-invested for the top gains.

The world's richest investor, Warren Buffett, follows this long-haul method. He picks enterprises which have risen slowly and steadily over the years. Usually they carry a famous brand name and pay punchy dividends. Wily Warren favours companies like Coca-Cola, Gillette and McDonalds. You don't necessarily have to be in at the beginning. Even companies which have a bumper share tag after pleasing the City for many years are expected to shine on through the years.

The strategy's proved to be safe so far, even though some of the world's biggest firms have been known to wobble. But it's a bit tedious if you do shares for fun as well as profit. The happiest follower, it seems to me, is someone who's not all fascinated by moods and swings and just wants to make money from shares in a comparatively secure way. It's not entirely safe, of course – no investment plan is: it's a myth that blue chips are unassailable. There are several instances when their share values have taken a drubbing, and recovery if it's started at all, has been painfully slow. Blue chips can burn in the pan, too.

A variation of the longest play policy is to hold your shares for a long, long time in essence, but to nip in and out of the market when they start bouncing around a bit. Not so long ago, a high street bank, which had been rising gradually for years, suddenly put on a spurt, picking up 25 per cent in five weeks. A natural reaction would be to rejoice momentarily, then leave the shares to continue their usual humdrum, unspectacular climb.

But it might be better to regard that sudden burst as being highly vulnerable to a nasty correction, sell the stock for a nice profit, then buy it back when, hopefully, they have subsided a bit. This way you stick to the much-adored long haul system in principle, while still making the odd few pounds from dashing in and out the market according to its peaks and troughs. Remember that even the most reliable, stolid shares are pushed around by hopelessly unpredictable markets. So keep a weather eye open for any glaring chances to dip in and out.

A PE Lesson

All shoppers look for good value. It's easy with potatoes. You can see what they look like and compare prices on other market stalls. It's a bit harder with toasters, washing machines and lawn mowers. And it's downright difficult with companies.

Yet all City analysts look for 'good value', i.e. spiffing quality shares at rock-bottom prices. It's not just a question of checking how much profit company accountants state in the annual report. 'Value' also depends on fine managers, future expectancies, public admiration of the brand, the condition of machinery, the state of the global economy and many more things. It's hard for private punters to determine the true worth of a company, or anything near it. But if you read the financial pages you may garner enough information to decide if a company is bringing home the goods. But even if it is, this still doesn't make a firm 'good value'. It's not a bargain if all its good points are already reflected in the share price. Top investors make their money by searching out good value companies which still have cheap shares after being overlooked by fellow punters.

This book isn't meant to go into all the technical ways of weighing up a company's value. But we ought to touch on a figure mentioned earlier (see the chapter Special Shares) called the PE. This stands for the price-to-earnings ratio. To arrive at the PE for a company, you divide the ordinary profits after tax by the number of shares in issue. (Ordinary profits are gains which aren't swollen by the sale of buildings and other assets.) I'm sorry if you're beginning to panic at all this complicated stuff, but bear with me. Very roughly speaking, the lower a company's PE, the better value the shares are. Working out the PE of a company is a chore. But you don't have to do it. Ask your broker what the PE is for a company which interests you, or look for it among share listings pages of the *Financial Times*. If you can find a company which has a PE lower than other enterprises in the same field, then it could be worth a punt.

Charting

Crystal balls don't work. You can't look into a company's future, more's the pity. But you can inspect its past. This is what chartists, or technical analysts, as they like to be called, do all the time. They

draw complicated-looking graphs to show an equity's ups and downs over a period of time. They use these to make projections into the future. If the share acts true to form, and you put your money on it, you're in clover. Trouble is history isn't supposed to repeat itself and just less than a third of my phalanx of expert informants think chartism is for the birds. The rest of them agree you can't predict the future by looking at the past – except, that is, in the peculiar world of shares. Past performance can be the key, they claim, to share price in the future. And the consensus view seems to be that while charts shouldn't be used as sure indicators on their own, it's all right to lump their results with other buy or sell signals.

You might imagine chartists simply draw straight lines to show whether a share is heading north or south, rather like those simple graphs you find on office walls in business cartoons. But they've turned it into a more complicated process than that. Chartists draw the basic line showing the shares progress, then they intersect it with other lines, curves and squiggles. The resulting diagrams don't tell an obvious story, and you need the skills and knowledge of a tea-leaf reader to make sense of them.

There's the 'head and shoulders', for instance. The principal line showing the share's progress forms two hills (shoulders) in the line with a larger bump in between them (the head). This configuration is a bad sign, apparently. Then there's the 'double top' when the main line forms two large hills on either side of a dip in the middle. It gets even more complicated with configurations called 'the four phases' and 'the flag'.

As this is a book of straightforward hints, we'll only pick out one of the easiest examples of chartism – the trend line. To use it, draw two lines at right angles on a piece of paper. Write 'share price' along the upright arm and 'time' along the bottom. Take a company you're interested in and mark its share prices on your diagram in a series of dots over three months. Now put a ruler along the dips in the line and join them up with a pencil. Does this new line head upwards or point downwards? This, according to chartists, will tell you whether the share will progress or decline in the next few months.

Where's the Action?

A classic City maxim is 'Go where the market strength is'. So if you read that property companies are taking off or banks are notching up high profits, you might sell stocks in some less-favoured domains of the market to build up your stake in buildings and banks.

True, one or two companies may be tripping the light fantastic in out-of-fashion sectors where everybody else is stumbling. But if you ignore that sector and instead buy shares in a more favoured territory, you will have a better chance of picking a winner – as nearly all shares in that sector are doing well. Conversely, if you invest in a business sector in which most firms are struggling, the bigger chance you have of becoming unstuck.

Better than Average

This plan was recommended by only a few of my City moles, but they insist it works. Most of their successes, though, have come about in blue-chip stocks. To work it, you'll need to know the average share rise of your chosen company over a twelve-month run. The easiest way to do this is to note down its share price on the first of each month, add them all up and divide by 12. (If in a hurry you could track the price for half a year, though your average would be less accurate.) Now look at how the share is performing today. Are the shares currently moving forward more strongly than the annual average which you've just worked out? If they are, it's reckoned to be a dandy sign for the future.

Winners and Losers

Page the Teletext 'Winners and Losers' feature. Next to each company on the screen is marked a rise or fall in its share price today. Next to this information, you're given a reason for the price change. It might be 'results delight City' or ' fall in demand' or 'rising pound'. Now ask yourself if one of the companies listed among the 'Losers' is similar to any enterprise in your portfolio. If so, the reason for a share plunge for the company on the screen (let's call it Company A) may also apply to the very similar firm in your portfolio. If your company hasn't experienced a nasty fall yet, does the fate of Company A suggest that it might happen soon? You could take this as an early warning and sell your stake before the big drop.

Playing Footsie

The Footsie, which turns the daily share changes of Britain's biggest 100 companies into one handy figure, was born in 1984. Before that, the main indicator of daily share prices was the FT 30 Share Index, based on the prices of the UK's top industrial and commercial companies. Nowadays, more weight is given to the Footsie as it's thought to be a better reflection of the modern switch from industry to service trades. And of course an average taken from 100 firms is more reliable than a sample of 30.

More interesting to share-choosers, though, is that once a company becomes important enough to join the Footsie, its share price usually makes a leap. One reason is that reaching this hallowed position is seen as a sure sign of success. The other, more down-to-earth explanation, is the existence of index tracker funds. These institutions, usually run by big unit trust combines, invest in every company in the Footsie. Then if the index rises (as it historically does over time) the fund rises too. For a tracker fund to stay a true tracker fund, its managers have to throw money at all companies in the index – and that includes any newcomers. So once a firm joins the Footsie, its shares will almost certainly rise as tracker fund managers rush to buy them.

If you read that a company may soon be grand enough to be listed in the Footsie, give it your consideration. Remember that by the time its membership is confirmed, it's probably too late. The other side to the coin is that every time a company puts its legs under the Footsie table, another is kicked out. If one of your companies is facing relegation, expect the shares to tumble.

Working the Time Difference

Rises or falls on Wall Street, the biggest, most influential securities market in the world, are usually mirrored on our Stock Exchange. There are several reasons for this, a significant one being that the average company in the Footsie 100 Index earns half its income abroad (surprising isn't it?).

Now let's look at an example of how this link with the USA might be made to work in favour of investors. New York is five hours behind London. Share prices over here are forging ahead, fuelled by the morning's news of a whacking great take-over. But during the afternoon here, it's the start of another day in Wall Street, and opening prices there are well down on rumours of a rise in interest rates. The London market's earlier improvement is rudely thumped into reverse. By close of play in Britain, the index is off by 25 points.

Wall Street falls much further towards the end of New York's working day (late evening here). It's down by 170 points at the close. This probably means a major fall in London stocks next day. Some investors will snap up those cheaper shares first thing, hoping that a depressed New York will bounce back when it opens during Britain's afternoon. Given the size of yesterday's slump, this isn't an unreasonable hope. If there is a sizeable rebound those stocks bought cheaply in the morning in London will become dearer by 4.15pm, when they can be sold at a profit. It might not be a very big return, but it's only taken a day to make it.

Now we'll look at a different way to benefit from the New York time difference. Shares in Britain dip on Monday morning and the Dow Jones Index also falls slightly on opening. But by the time the London market has closed at 4.30pm, the USA shares react to happy trade figures and shoot upwards to close 120 points ahead. Some punters will sell shares when these gains are reflected in London next day. Around 4.15pm our time, when New York is once more underway, the Dow Jones might well fall again, having over-heated the day before. On the London exchange, early sellers now re-purchase their stock at cheaper prices.

There are a couple of snags to these cunning plans. First you must be prepared to risk quite a lot of money to make the exercise worthwhile, because profits over a 24-hour interval are rarely very high (if they are made at all). Secondly, you'll have to take account of one stamp duty, two lots of dealing charges and the difference between buying and selling prices.

The Bond Effect

Bonds are traded like stocks and shares, though they're outside the scope of this book. However, many wily share-pickers keep a beady eye on the bond market. They can influence equities. Theoretically, if bonds are up, shares follow and if bonds stumble, so do shares. There's a handy time gap which works in the investor's favour, though. So if your newspaper tells you that bonds are strong, you could expect equities to climb some time later. This gap is calculated at between three and 12 months. It would be nice if it could be tied down to a more specific period, but anybody who expects consistency from the financial markets is bananas. The relationship between bonds and equities is fickle. Treat it as another possible indicator – but don't bank on it.

The Option Option

Instead of shares, you can buy options to buy shares. (They're known as 'traded equity options'.) It's a complicated rigmarole with its own tips for success, and needs another book to do the subject justice. But like bonds, there's a soothsaying aspect to options which ordinary share enthusiasts can home in on. Many investors monitor the traded options market in the hope that its movements up or down will provide insights on how the stock market will behave in future.

Options come in two forms: 'calls' or 'puts'. Punters who buy calls expect the shares of an enterprise, usually a leading corporation, to rise. If they don't ascend to reach a target price, holders of calls can lose all their investment. People who shop for puts wouldn't be at all downhearted at this, because they only make a profit if the shares tumble. Conveniently, the *Financial Times* totals the number of calls and puts bought daily. If calls outnumber puts, expectations are high that the Footsie will rise. But if puts are cornering the market, then a lot of investors obviously feel otherwise.

A drawback to this reasoning is that the options market trades simultaneously with the stock market. So investors who dabble in options have no more information to draw on than those who put their trust in proper shares. However, there's a perception that people who dabble in options are more likely to be right than share buyers. This is because option devotees not only have to be right – they have to be very right. It's argued, therefore, that a bit more careful thought may go into option trades, making the option market view that bit more accurate. Also, options are a favourite with big institutions and, as we know, they pay fortunes for the best information from analysts. This should also turn the options market into a good-quality indicator.

So far we've only looked at the option market as a whole. But sometimes a press report on the previous day's option sales will mention a particular company by name. It might say: 'Bloggs Bearings was the darling of buyers today with thousands of call options traded.' This shows a lot of confidence in Bloggs Bearings and you could take this as an indication that its shares might rise. After all, a lot of option buyers certainly think so. Conversely, if the paper reports that more put options were traded in Bloggs than any other company, then evidently the company's chances of increasing its share values aren't rated.

Two Good Signs

You may read that a company is arranging a number of meetings with City analysts and the fund managers of unit trusts, investment trusts and insurance giants. This is a common practice of directors who believe their shares are undervalued by the market. They invite the big wigs who drive the stock market to come and see how well they're doing. Their hope is that the visitors will be impressed and revise their expectations or buy huge blocks of shares, thus raising the company's value. And incidentally boosting the worth of the directors' holdings or share options.

You don't have to attend its show-off junkets to know that a firm is pretty pleased with itself and that the shares may be worth buying. (Would 'open days' be arranged if the company was in trouble?) If you decide to act on a press report that meetings have been arranged, you'll probably be able to buy shares before the fund managers who are invited. Even if these big spenders are bowled-over with the company's performance and prospects, they may not be able to buy stock straight away. They'll probably seek permission first. As always, the private investor, a law unto himself, can act faster –a bit like Drake's tiny ships running rings round the Armada.

The Nice One

You're watching a current affairs programme on TV. A captain of industry is asked his opinion about interest rates or sterling exchange rates. He has a winning smile, an attractive personality, confidence brims over. Moreover facts and figures are ceaselessly tossed out, indicating he's well informed. He talks sense, too. The fellow guest who disagrees with him is eloquently and firmly brought round to his view. You're impressed. And you know he's only been invited on to the programme because the producer is sure his contributor knows his stuff.

A company with this kind of person at the helm is lucky. Directors who can impress at first sight are rare. They'll secure orders and make deals by winning over others, just as they've impressed you. Find out if the firm he leads is quoted on the Stock Exchange. Are the shares rising? You could be on to a good thing.

Next day the managing director of a company in which you own shares is being interviewed on Radio Four's *Today* programme. He won't give a direct answer to ticklish questions. He flounders, ums and ers, becomes rattled once or twice – and doesn't he seem shifty? Yet the rest of the board must tolerate him. Are they as bad as he is? Of course, the MD may be a shy saint who simply comes across badly. But that doesn't solve the problem that he'll seem incompetent if not shady to the people he hopes to sell his products to. That can bode ill for the share price.

As mentioned before I don't entirely agree with all the advice I've been given for this book. And I'm not sure I'm happy to assess company directors on their image, rather than track record. As a journalist, I've met scores of tricksters and villains. The most outrageous of them seemed very plausible, nice men and women. This is how they're able to con people. An attractive persona is part of their stock in trade.

Wizard Wheezes

All wise share-pickers have grand plans. This does not stop them having strategies within their exalted design. But lower down the ladder still come the wheezes. They are all part of the successful investor's tool kit. Here are some of them.

.

The Leaders and Laggards Game

If you look in Saturday's edition of the *Financial Times* you'll see a list of the week's 'leaders and laggards'. This tells you which sectors of the market, as opposed to individual companies, are enjoying improved share prices and which sectors are trailing the field. It might say that, on average, retail stores are doing well or that oil exploration companies are generally struggling. If one store excels then you might expect that it has one particular quality which helps it make more money than its peers. But if all stores are doing well – and the FT says they are – then you could assume that the reason is common to all big shops and that we're seeing a national surge in customer confidence.

Having made the assumption that cash tills are tinkling all over the high street, all you need do now is find a store whose share price lags behind the rest. If the theory works, the shares will soon show an increase – after you've bought a piece of the action.

Alternatively, should you hold shares in a sector listed among the 'laggards' in the *Financial Times*, you are entitled to hear alarm bells. If a company in which you hold equities hasn't yet fallen with the rest of its sector you still have time to hit the lifeboats.

A difficulty with this theory is that sectors listed among the 'laggards' today may appear with the 'leaders' next week. This is because falling balls bounce back, as we've seen. And, of course, today's leaders may soon become 'laggards', bearing in mind their vulnerability to profit-taking. So it's wise to keep a check of the 'leaders and laggards' column over more than one week before buying or selling.

Follow that Firm

In business, it's normal to fly like an eagle even when surrounded by turkeys. Companies whose share price consistently betters others in the same sector are known as ' market leaders'. Others in the same sphere flounder around, their shares slowly haemorrhaging away, while the top dog makes slow, steady progress. Market leaders simply do the job better than anyone else. They have usually been around a long time. They often have strong brand names and their branches seem to be everywhere. You can buy their shares when they've already doubled in the last 12 months and still expect to make money. They are usually worth following.

Stag Parties

When a company decides to raise cash by floating on the Stock Exchange it may offer shares to the public at a fixed price. Depending on how popular is the offer, that price either rises or falls on the first day of trading. In City parlance, a 'stag' is somebody who buys newly-issued shares in the hope of selling for profit as soon as they come on the open market. For a would-be stag to turn a quick profit, he needs to guess which way the cookie is set to crumble before he lashes out on shares. The press will write up their opinion on the subject before the last date to send your money off. In my experience they're not often wrong. This is not so much due to journalistic skills as the peculiar power of prophecy. If readers are told a share is likely to trade at a premium on its first day, they buy it in large numbers – and it duly rises. If the press says the offer isn't alluring, readers will be put off and the price will tumble on its first outing. The message is simple – do what the papers say.

24 Hours Cloning

This system works when the market's in an optimistic phase and shares are rising daily. You scan yesterday's performance of the top 100 shares and make believe that exactly the same thing will happen today. This imaginary 'performance' is meant to help you choose which shares to buy and which to sell.

We all know that today's prices won't track yesterday's exactly. But assuming the 'bull run' continues, most shares will still be rising, and those firms that were particularly favoured yesterday may easily be popular today. If a share rose 35p yesterday, you could buy it first thing and sell just before 4.30pm hoping for a repeat performance. It might not reach 35p again of course, but a smaller rise would still realise a useful gain. It's not at all unusual for shares to rise five days on the trot, but you do run the risk of bad news or profit-taking, which would send your chosen share back to whence it came.

Another upsetter of the apple-cart would be if a bear (falling) market suddenly sets in. But then no system can allow for a complete turnabout in fortunes and you'd have to accept that risk. Often, however, a change from a bull to a bear market starts the day's trading. This would just give you time to see how the wind blows before acting. However, it must be said that some investors dislike index cloning because the gains are small in relation to outlay. You also need the time and patience to watch teletext all day to be alert to a dreaded sea-change.

Corrections

When the Footsie pushes against an old ceiling or breaks through to record heights, even optimists doubt this happy state will last more than another day or two. It hardly ever does. It is soon realised that equities have become oversold and the rot sets in. Occasionally late-comers, who jubilantly scramble on the raft in the last few stages of a bull run, suddenly find themselves plunging down a vertical waterfall. Any substantial fall after a rapid climb is known as a correction (less likely to cause a panic than calling it a disaster).

Though the term 'correction' suggests a sensible and inevitable sort of thing to happen, predicting one in time to save yourself losses is as difficult as telling a female butterfly from the male. There are, however, a few possible signals. To begin with, it's worth monitoring the current Wall Street performance. When New York sneezes the rest of the world catches cold. Trouble is an overnight correction on the Dow is often reflected in London before the Stock Exchange opens. So private investors can't really take advantage, though a mini-crash on Wall Street first thing would affect our later afternoon market and it may be possible for more alert investors to sell in time. (Exploiting the transatlantic time difference is explored elsewhere in the book.) You may also find some dire predictions about a possible correction in the papers, based perhaps on warnings about rate rises or growing inflation. Bull runs are assailable to both factors.

Some investors anticipate a correction after a two per cent rise in the Footsie and act accordingly. Or they give a bull run four days and then brace themselves for a plunge. But both approaches are based on unreliable history and, as always, it's best to stay flexible. If there are valid causes why a surge in share prices should be sustained, like falling inflation, rising unemployment or growing interest rates, then four days of consecutive record-breaking could easily stretch into six. (The all-time record as I write is 11.) If however there are no stunning reasons why shares should be entering rarefied realms, four days may be too long to go before you begin selling.

Single Company Corrections

When the fear of a correction doesn't stalk the entire market, it still skulks behind corners to threaten individual companies. Even without a dose of bad news, any share which rises too fast and far can burn up in the upper reaches and plummet back to earth. City professionals will say an overbought share is 'overheating' or becoming 'toppy'. When its new fancy price no longer reflects the real value, a correction is usually imminent. You might also want to check shares of companies in the same sector to see if they have already been affected by a correction. Because if so, your company's fortunes may soon slip in sympathy.

It's easy to see a correction as an adversity. But if you're in an acquisitive mood, it can be a boon. It gives you the chance of snaffling more shares for your money. You may see a correction in a kindlier light if you refer to it by its other name – 'buying opportunity'.

Some highly-regarded investors won't sell if they feel a correction is imminent. They prefer to ride the storm, confident that a good quality stock will overcome all market set-backs – if it's held for long enough.

A Big Deal in the Dodgy City

It's an exciting day in share-land. A smallish firm has done a deal with a prestigious corporate giant with a household name. Such a pact can send shares in the lesser concern up like a sky-rocket. Either that or the share's price will improve Roman candle fashion – in small daily bursts. A common path for a share to take in these welcome circumstances is for it to rise, quick as a wink, by 50 per cent. Then it falters and falls by 10 per cent. After a couple of days, it gets a second wind, rising again until it reaches a 60 per cent level above its original price. After reaching this zenith (known as its 'closing resistance' in the trade) the share begins to decay, quite slowly, until it settles at a level which is not much better than the starting price.

Why should this pattern be established? Well, it happens because on first news of the deal, the City is thrilled. It seems like a rich opportunity for the small company and a bonanza for its shareholders. But then analysts and journalists reach for their magnifying glasses and decide, after a few days' study, that a link-up between David and Goliath might not work out for all sorts of reasons. So enthusiasm tails off.

The question is, how can we be sure that the share price has reached its final high, so that we can sell for a maximum profit? We can't of course. But a number of City specialists suggest that you should consider cashing your chips not more than four or five days after the deal is declared, as the delights of a honeymoon seldom last longer. If you hold shares in the lesser company before the news breaks and sell afterwards, you can always renew your loyalty by buying them back when they settle back to their old level. After all, in the fullness of time, the new deal might work out very well indeed.

It's a Funny Thing About Shares

I don't imagine I need tell you that things in the share world aren't always what they seem. You are probably exasperated by the way shares rise like an oil gusher when you expect them to fall like a diving bell, and vice versa. Some of these mysteries can be explained by City observers and some can't – though they will always try (after the event, usually). Let me show you some of the less obvious ways in which shares travel – and how you may be able to benefit from them.

The Barrier Harrier

Used car dealers know all about mental barriers in their particular numbers game. If a vehicle has 79,998 miles on the clock, they can ask a fatter price than if it has travelled another three miles to record 80,001 miles. Share dealing is also about second-hand goods.

If an equity is priced at £1.99 it often seems hard to break through something known as 'round figure resistance' to reach £2. The difficulty is that many punters will have resolved not to sell their holding until the share reaches £2. So the action comes to a full stop against this brick wall and sometimes bounces back with the shock. A wise investor might decide that the psychological wall is a nuisance and sell at £1.99. He will almost certainly save time.

Psychological barriers also come into play when shares are moving in a downwards direction. Let's take a share which has dropped from £3.50 to £3.03. The barrier in this case is £3. You could regard it as a buffer in the path of a runaway train. If the share is not falling fast enough to destroy the buffer it will probably come to rest against it. If it's going to rise, this could be the time. But if the train crashes through the £3 buffer, perhaps you should expect the fall to continue for a while yet. So with little hope of a recovery for the time being, you might consider cutting losses by selling the share.

You often hear psychological barriers mentioned in the same breath as the Footsie index. The comment: 'Shares again failed to break through that all-important 5,000 psychological barrier,' is a journalists' cliché. If the index hovers around 4,980 points, say, it can't seem to splash through the 5,000 watershed. But once it does, oh boy! Rather like a released elastic band, the market can zing upwards for a time. However, the surge often doesn't last and it seems a mite easier for the Footsie to break through a psychological barrier if it's travelling backwards.

A Penny Block

There are many other mental hurdles at work in the investor's world. Another example is when a penny share tumbles from double into single figures. While a 10p share sounds as though it has some value, a fall to 9p seems a bit serious. Inversely, a share valued for years at 9p which one day edges to 10p feels more positive than the situation probably merits. Yet it may encourage more speculators, perhaps sparking a further improvement to 13.5p – a handsome gain of 50 per cent. Yet the underlying reason for the initial shift of 1p to 10p might be very slight indeed. The more cautious investor would refuse to leap on this sort of bandwagon, even if the music is sweet for a time, because the rising share isn't supported by facts. Speculators, as opposed to investors, would be tempted, but would need to be nifty to nip in and out the market before the beginning of the end.

The Season Reason

A firm in your portfolio sends you its half-time report. It seems they made a small loss over six months. You conclude the directors have lost their touch and resolve to part company. But wait! The firm makes hose-pipes and garden furniture, doesn't it? The figures before you are for October to March. When the annual report comes out, covering the summer period, that loss is going to turn to a profit. Check last year's figures to see if I'm right.

Hopefully your fellow shareholders will realise the seasonal nature of the business and not begin to unload. Otherwise the share price will slide for no good reason, putting off other investors and starting a vicious circle. Though if this happens you could always take advantage of the cheaper shares to hoist your stake. But before you throw your money about, you might try to get hold of a long-term weather forecast.

There are many seasonal businesses whose profit-and-loss accounts don't reflect true progress when they're published at the company's 'wrong time of year'. They include makers of ice-cream, cycles, yachts, lawn-mowers, seeds, and fizzy drinks. But don't forget some less obvious candidates, like the motor trade which sells most cars in August. In the case of holiday companies you might expect their profits to sparkle more in the summer, but the growing trade in skiing holidays and winter breaks makes seasonal differences in turnover less significant. Also many bookings for summer are made just after Christmas when deposits or full fees are paid. Shop takings are strongly affected by seasonal fluctuations. By far the healthiest selling comes in the run-up to Christmas followed by the January sales. Toy makers, card designers and book publishers also sell most of their stock at this time of year.

Experienced investors become rather worried if a company's normal seasonal pattern goes haywire. If it does better in winter than in summer, when the trading pattern is normally the other way round, there's a chance of trouble ahead. If this happens – and profits overall are uninspiring – you may want to consider your position, i.e. jump ship.

The Protection Racket

National economies are fragile and neurotic. They are easily knocked off balance bringing in the cold wind of depression. When that blows all companies take some sort of pounding. Expect small ventures to suffer more than their seniors on the premise that it's easier to gust a fishing boat off course than an oil tanker. Yet nobody's safe. Shares in giant companies are also buffeted by high inflation, rising interest rates and lack of customer confidence. But don't let the fear of an economic slump send you scurrying out of the stock market back into a building society. Take refuge in some of the areas of business which are more insulated from a recession than others. Whatever happens, the public can't seem to do without their products. It's wise to have securities of some of these less fallible companies stuffed away in your portfolio.

Healthcare comes top of the 'protected' list. Pills and potions are among the last purchases we're prepared to go without when our income slips. And hospital equipment is so vital that it sells well during the worst kind of slump.

Staple foods like bread and milk are items we can't do without, so bakery and dairy firms are resilient to economic stagnation. Meat processors aren't though, as we switch to cheaper foods. Neither are supermarkets, as customers stop buying luxuries.

The sale of so-called white goods, like washing machines, dish washers and fridges do slide, as do orders for TV sets, hi-fi, furniture and DIY materials. House builders, estate agents, property companies and package-tour operators are badly treated by economic stagnation, too. So if you see another recession looming up, avoid shares in firms which supply goods that, if push comes to shove, people can do without.

The Inflation Tool

A bull run, where the Footsie breaks new ground every day, is often fired by good news about inflation. It's not low inflation which keeps shares bubbling along nicely. What really seems to matter is a mass feeling that the monthly data will get even better as the year goes on. But if there's the smallest whisper of inflation turning upwards, the markets will start to turn down. What might really send it crashing, though, is if rising unemployment suddenly changes to rising employment. You might think it a bit odd that an improvement on the jobs front should weaken the money markets. If people find it easier to win work, you might expect their extra spending power to bring in more profits all round. But more jobs tends to stoke inflation because bosses have to increase wages to attract workers. If your newspaper tells you inflation is set to rise you might care to become liquid (not literally, of course; it's City speak for swapping shares for cash).

On Your Cycle

You may be surprised how old is the wonderful world of shares. Stocks and, even more surprisingly, share options were certainly traded in the Middle Ages. Shares may have even existed before that. The first public companies in Britain were the Muscovy and East India Companies. As early as 1553, Muscovy stockholders caught a cold with a doomed voyage by Sebastian Cabot to find a north east trade route to China. But partakers in the East India Company became the first truly happy investors. They were making about 40 per cent a year out of silk and spice sailings to the Orient. (Piratical attacks by Captain Kidd notwithstanding.)

The number of public companies grew and by 1697 there was a special act licensing stock brokers to strut their stuff in coffee shops and alley ways of London. Stock brokers flouting the rules were troubled by flying fruit in another kind of stocks for three days at a time.

From the middle of the 19th century, statistical boffins, probably more interested in pure mathematics than getting rich like us, have studied market movements for recurring patterns of booms and busts. At least one search is reputed to have gone back to the year 1260. Over the centuries, these academics have picked out a number of 'market cycles' – the time between a market peak and a trough which repeats itself over the years. The worth of a cycle is that it could help you decide whether to hang on to your shares because prices are generally advancing, or to abandon ship because a fall seems due.

Nevertheless, some of these cycles are so long – up to 60 years in one case – that you need to go way back in the records to stand a chance of profiting. As one aim of this book is to help you make educated guesses without doing too much work we'll ignore the longest cycle. (Its discoverer Nikolai Kondratieff, a Russian, didn't live long enough to see a practical demonstration of his cycle. Working on it was deemed to be an unacceptable face of capitalism by his Communist government. He was sent to the Gulag where he died, aged 38, in solitary confinement.)

Maybe the most practical cycle from the ordinary investor's view point is called the Kitchin Wave, after the Harvard professor who discovered it. Professor Kitchin estimated that it takes about 40 months for a high and low point on the stock market to go full circle. First published in the 1920s, the Kitchin cycle has since been revised to encompass about four years.

If you put faith in this cycle – and many experts do – let's look at how you might profit by it. You calculate that the stock market has been pushing forwards, give or take the odd stumble, for two years. The Kitchin cycle predicts it will now start retracing steps – taking a total of four years to complete the circle. So you might consider taking your money out towards the end of the two year bull run. If, however, the market has been rising for 21 months, you still have three months to make hay. But if the index has been falling for 20 months, the cycle tells you to be chary of shelling out for any more shares for another four months.

It's probably not a wholesome wheeze to rely solely on a cycle before selling or buying huge parcels of stock. This is especially true if the current market trend is clearly against it. But taken with other indicators, the cycle may be useful. Here's an example: the Footsie is breaking all records, but a rise in interest rates is rumoured and bubbling inflation threatens. These are both bad signs and press columnists prophesy the end of the bull run. If the cycle says so, too, you might want to pull on your selling boots.

But why should we put any faith in the Kitchin cycle or in any cycle? After all, they're worked out with data from the past. And where's the law that history must repeat itself? Well, there may be some strange market forces at work which nobody's nailed down yet. For instance, have mysterious rays from outer space got anything to do with it? Sounds barmy, until you realise that sunspot activity, which also occurs at regular intervals, is believed to affect crop harvests. The success or failure of harvests can and do affect the global economy which in turn sways share prices in the Square Mile. William Jevons, a distinguished Victorian economist, dug out an 11-year market cycle in the 1800s which he attributed to sunspot activity.

Other scholars have worked out long, sophisticated economic cycles. But there are many simpler (and more useful) 'pop cycles' in existence. The best of these have been brought to my attention by the phalanx of City professionals who've supplied hints for this book.

The Quick Quick Slow Cycle

In New York, it's been noticed that two good years side-by-side are often followed by a poor third year. Average prices need to rise by more than a fifth for this to happen. Sometimes the third dismal session has been lousy indeed. The years 1929, 1937 and 1974 all saw inauspicious declines. As usual, we can expect changes on the Dow Jones Index to waft across the Atlantic. So if the Footsie enjoys two cracking years, you might deem it prudent to turn some of your shares into cash for year three.

The President's Cycle

A host of serious investors have noticed this phenomenon -- and have shown me figures to back it up. The evidence is that shares perform well in America during election years, but do badly in the following 12 months. Once again as New York is so closely linked with London, this cycle is worth a gander.

A closer look at the evidence for the president's cycle is that prices for the year after the election don't really go into free fall, but do swing wildly about. This isn't a bad thing for investors who like to dip in and out. As we've seen, it's when prices are volatile that most opportunities occur for making a fast buck. There is, by the way, a peculiar exception to that bit about the year after the election being a disappointment. It doesn't seem to apply to years ending in a five.

At Fives and Sevens

This is another transatlantic trend which has an effect, though perhaps not as pronounced, on our markets. Investors have caught on to a tendency for Wall Street shares to do better in years ending in five and worse in those finishing with a seven. Alternate seventh years are exceptionally rotten. 1957 was wretched and so was 1977.

The Election Wave

Long before a parliamentary election, Stock Exchange prices will be adjusted depending on which party stands the best chance of winning. So in the days approaching polling day, unless there's a major scandal, you wouldn't expect politics to affect the Footsie in the slightest. Yet in the week before an election, share values nearly always rally. This has happened in 11 out of 13 general elections since 1950. The biggest gush of enthusiasm came in 1974 when the FT All-Share index added nearly four per cent in the last few days. That year we elected a parliament with no overall majority. On the only two occasions when the stock market fell just before polling, Labour got in.

Why should belated pre-election jumps happen? You would imagine the sensible course for investors would be to wait and see who wins. Well, though most of us deny it, it seems that private investors have a bit of the gambler in them and can't resist a punt on a big event. They simply must have a late fling on the outcome. So they buy shares in companies which should do particularly well out of Labour policies or in companies which will benefit from a Tory victory.

If the outcome seems predictable, as it was for Labour in 1997, then last-minute doubts creep in. Earlier, Tony Blair had announced plans for a windfall tax on privatised companies. This burden had been factored into share prices long before the election. But if the Tories were re-elected, then there'd be no windfall tax, and shares in utilities and other privatised giants would shoot up. Some braver investors thought it worth a gamble on the outside chance of the Tories scraping home. They bought heavily into privatisation shares and the market posted gains.

There's also conjecture that share prices lift immediately before an election out of sheer good spirits born of a realisation that a boring campaign is about to end. So as most money is made by investors who ignore the crowd, the best advice is: don't buy in the five days before an election when prices may be artificially high. While if you're considering selling a parcel of shares, do it on polling day.

Some investors have a play-safe tactic for use during the run-up to a general election. As the markets can gallop about wildly up and down on both sides of polling day, they will sell some stock in the month before voting takes place. Then, depending on the result, they can either repurchase their holdings or sell even more shares after the result.

Boom Rats and Ox Tails

I avoid trading in Far East markets. This may be a mistake as lots of Europeans make money here. But, as this book suggests, I put huge dollops of faith in mass psychology and its effects on shares. As I regret having no experience of Eastern people, it's rather hard to apply such principles to their financial markets. However, for those who are interested in the Japanese Nikkei Index, it might be useful to know that the Year of the Rat is often a boom year, while the Year of the Ox can be a bummer.

Buyer Beware

One of the jewels of advice in my collection from share experts is: 'The way to make profits is to avoid losses.' Fine, you already know that. But what I think they mean by this seemingly obvious maxim is that it's no good rejoicing over your winners if they're overwhelmed by losses. Most of the contributors feel that knowing how to avoid dogs is actually more important in the long run than picking thoroughbreds. I don't entirely agree because the profits from choosing a winning share are, in theory anyway, unlimited. It's far from unknown for a share to multiply by 10 times in a year (this is known as a 'tenbagger', by the way, and very nice it is too). But while a triumphant share can improve by 1000 per cent or more, a truly disastrous stock can only cost you your whole stake at worst – a total loss of 100 per cent. But still there's no denying a dipping share is something we'd all rather do without. Here are some ways to spot companies you might care to avoid.

Naughty, Naughty. . .

Think twice about investing in a company which has ever been in trouble for breaking rules of the Stock Exchange, a financial watchdog, a trade association, a quango or any other body. The firm's least sin will be carelessness – and who wants to trust money in a slipshod outfit? Sometimes, though, guilty executives who made the mistakes resign or are ousted from the company. This

106

gives the remaining team a better chance of heaving on the company boot straps. Meanwhile, the scandal is sure to have depressed share prices which may now be in the bargain basement. You might want to buy shares for a ride to recovery.

Un-Green, Un-Green

Perhaps you should hesitate before entrusting your brass to companies making or selling stuff which harms the environment. Even

if you see no wrong in their activities, other people will. A throng of placard-waving, chanting protesters outside the hall on annual meeting day does nothing for share prices. Also, many less ardent members of the public will be boycotting the company's goods at the supermarket. And what about the future of a company with an environment-unfriendly reputation? Most older people weren't encouraged to think much about the worst effects of thoughtless industry on the planet, so don't always give the subject much weight. But youngsters have the dangers rammed home to them in school and on children's TV. Even some of those dreadful American cartoons cast polluting industrialists as baddies.

A company which still tests on animals may also face serious trouble in the future. Growing numbers of the public object to lab assistants putting chemicals in rabbits' eyes. The directors of an animal-testing company may be about to change their ways, but if there are no visible signs, step aside.

When Cheap is Dear

If we could all recognise which shares really are bargains, it would be a wonderful world. Back-breaking research, the latest computer technology and high-grade number-crunching by highly paid analysts give fund managers the edge in this quest but a detailed search is beyond the resources of a private investor.

For those who haven't done the necessary donkey work, there is a temptation to think a share's cheap because it is cheap. But in the share world, cheap and inexpensive aren't the same thing. Not at all. In my first three months as an investor, I bought a thousand pounds' worth of shares in a company for 2p each. And I persuaded my dad to spend £300 on them, too. I was so ignorant about this firm, I hadn't a clue what they did. I just assumed that a tuppenny share couldn't fall much further, but could rise quite a lot. How wrong! What happened is that share did even worse and to stop it vanishing up its own assets, the firm divided everybody's shares by 10. This meant the share value rose to 20p, but now everybody had a tenth as many shares for their money. Then the shares started to drift back again, penny by penny, until my investment began to look very sick indeed. I found, too late, that often happens to low-cost shares. There are two lessons to be learned from this tale. Shares aren't necessarily a bargain if they're at a bargain price. And if you give your dad a duff tip, be prepared for a total lack of parental forgiveness – for ever. I still keep my pesky certificate as an awful warning, rather like a farmer leaves a dead crow hanging in a wheat field to scare other birds.

Time to Bail Out

Always knowing the exact moment to say goodbye to companies in his portfolio would make any investor delirious with untold wealth. Sadly this is about as likely as receiving the bounty of a *Financial Times* from two years in the future. However, here are a few hints which may help you decide when enough is enough.

The first hurdle to overcome is the natural urge never to uncurl your fingers on a batch of shares once you've bought them. Most of us are driven (by optimism more than pride) to stick with our choices through thick and thin. To overcome this psychological nuisance, it helps to remember one of the oldest maxims to haunt the Stock Exchange, 'Nobody ever went broke taking a profit.' This means that once you've built up a reasonable profit, you should realise your shares are not as cheap as they were – and there may now be better bargains on offer. Time to sell the shares you have and buy those cut-price equities.

Trouble is there is another equally-often quoted City proverb which says quite the opposite: 'Always run your profits', meaning: 'If a share has done well so far, hang on in there.' This also seems like a sensible strategy – until you try to explain it to somebody who made £10,000 on a share and wished he'd sold it before it keeled over backwards, headed back down again, and eventually cost him £20,000. Well, do you sell a share which has provided enough wherewithal for a tropical holiday, or do you keep it in the

110

hope of even more delectable rewards? Should we? Shouldn't we? Here are some hints on the question given to me by people who are well versed in this particular Stock Exchange game. Some may help you to sell at the right time, some could stop you selling at the wrong time.

Half the Cake

One handy ploy is to call your broker once your holding doubles in price, but ask her to sell only half of it. This way you keep your cake and eat it: you can never lose your stake though you still take part in the action. You can enjoy what the trade calls 'a free ride'. And if the roller-coaster comes off the tracks later on, you won't lose a thing.

But don't make 'selling on a double' a hard and fast rule. If the share's upward charge shows no sign of slowing down, it doesn't make sense to kill the golden goose by pulling out. On the other hand, if your selection runs out of steam after a 60 per cent hike, say, and refuses to budge, it may not be worth waiting around for it to reach the full 100 per cent increase. You could sell half your stake on a 60 per cent improvement instead. If it then takes off sharply in a southerly direction, you should sell the rest.

Right now it's worth pointing out that you don't need two share certificates to sell half your stake in a company. You can dispose of as many of your equities as you like. Simply send in the certificate for all your shares to your broker after telling him how many you want to part with. You will later be posted a new certificate showing the number of shares you still have left.

The Seven Per Cent Solution

Many investors use this strategy. It has its attractions but calls for sturdy discipline. Here's a typical situation. Your share makes steady progress over a week or two after some encouraging news. It reaches a plateau, wobbles and begins to shed a few pence. Your instinct is to cash in your chips now. But what if this is only a resting point on a longer climb? Should you hang on – or not? The seven per cent solution relieves you of the agony of decision. You wait till the share reaches a peak and starts its fall. When it's tumbled by 7 per cent of its price at the peak, phone in a 'sell' order.

But why should we take a fall of seven per cent as the benchmark? Why not choose five per cent or 10 per cent? There's no real answer. But losing seven per cent of the profits you might have made if you'd sold at the very top (some hopes) doesn't seem too bad. However, if you wait until the price falls by a tenth then you're left nursing a loss which, for most of us, is big enough to hurt. You could be more cautious and settle on five per cent as the cut-off point, but this doesn't give you much of a margin if the share suddenly pulls up its pants and reaches for the sky again. A more speculative investor with high hopes for the company might increase her stop limit to 15 or even 20 per cent, but this may be pushing your luck a bit too far.

One-Year Itchers

It takes a very loyal shareholder to stand by her managers of a company if a share price decays over a long period and never shows the slightest sign of switching from reverse gear. But how long should you wait before giving it up as a bad job? Most of my experts say your patience can honourably run out after a year. But if the company's annual reporting day isn't too far off and the share happens to be steady at the time, rather than in its usual falling mode, you might as well wait a few more weeks. But as a rule, 12 months of floundering in the mire is probably long enough. If the share stops dwindling though and attains a steady, if uninspiring level, for six months or more, then it changes status and becomes a 'stagnant pool' (described in the chapter Share Categories) so hang on. There may be fireworks ahead.

To sum up then. Never cringe away from cutting out the dead wood, if only to release your funds for more promising fare. If a share has done nothing for you for a year, then it probably deserves the chop. But it's still worth looking at carefully before making an automatic decision. If you really can't understand why a black sheep in your fold isn't about to mend its ways and live up to its earlier promise, it would be judicious to extend the 12-month time limit.

Bad News Bears

This is a sad story. A company which has added value to your portfolio for years suddenly loses the magic. There are worrying signs. Sales and profits are down, running costs are up, debts are mounting. Then a key manager is head-hunted by a competitor. A well-known firm of brokers expresses public doubts. You can stay loyal if you like. But if the supply of bad news keeps a-coming, it's fair to wonder what other skeletons skulk in office cupboards. Popular wisdom is that there's always even worse to come, before things get better. Even if it's only for the sake of your nerves, you might want to think about waving bye-bye.

Nothing Doing

You hold shares in a company which has not swallowed up any smaller fish for years now. No letter comes through the door spelling out proposals for the purchase of another similar enterprise. Yet you know that making acquisitions is a classic way to grow and make greater profits. Can you really believe that no satisfactory targets have presented themselves for ages now? Or do you suspect that your directors aren't trying? One tactic here is to ring up the company's chief executive or chairman. Ask if any firms are currently in his gun-sights. He's not allowed to tell you under the insider trading rules, but he may give a plausible story why expansion would be silly at the moment. After all, many a board of directors has overreached itself by buying smaller businesses in haste. But if the chairman blusters on the phone and gives lame excuses, you should come over all grumpy. Use a few expressions like 'disappointing lethargy' and 'lack of action.' Then think about putting your money somewhere else.

Who's Running the Shop?

If you fly in a sleek modern jumbo jet you need to know that the pilot is well-trained, awake and wants to get there. If not, you would try to sell your tickets or not buy them in the first place. If you sail in a rust bucket or a clapped out steamer, you might still be willing to buy passage if a respected and responsible captain and a diligent, super-intelligent mate were at the helm. In shares, as in transport, you are a lot safer if the people in charge are of the first water. Here are some good reasons why you should test the talents of the directors who you are entrusting your share money to.

The Family Way

Some companies floated on the Stock Exchange are still largely run by members of one family. Such an outfit is worth a second look because its directors may be less inclined to feather their own desk at the expense of the firm as a whole. They're also less likely to sell out to any entrepreneurs with a darker side. Moreover, there's an incentive for directors to work longer hours in a long-

established family business which should bring a glow to the profit account.

A true family firm also has a bit of extra protection against going under completely. There's invariably a devastating sense of loss and an overwhelming blow to tradition and pride when such firms founder. So superhuman efforts will be made to stop it ever happening.

However, there is a snag which sometimes bedevils family firms and can bring them to ruin. It's possible there may be some out-dated ideas at work for which an aged patriarch is responsible. He could be too set in his ways to discard 'the old way of doing things'. An attitude like this may spell disaster for shareholders. Fortunately, though it's as well to be aware of the danger, it's probable that the stock character of 'overbearing father in the boardroom' isn't as common in real life as some old films and TV dramas would have us believe.

Chief Executives

If you study the page of a company report which gives a potted biography of the directors, you may notice that some of them also dignify the boardrooms of quite different firms. It's not unusual for managers to share their talents round in this way. Is there a danger then that they're concentrating too much on a business you have no interest in, at the expense of one in which you have? Well, they doubtless have their favourite. But even if this is not your company, it probably doesn't matter too much as ordinary directors don't have much say-so in the running of the firm.

But what if the chief executive or chairman in charge of your investment has other fish to fry? He may put the biggest share of his energies into another enterprise. This is unsettling because, as you sit by your swimming pool sipping a gin and tonic, you need to know that someone at the top is working fingers to the bone on your behalf. It's for this reason some investors will only touch firms whose top brass give their talents exclusively.

Fat Cats?

Before you leap into a new company, find out how much the directors are paid (it's usually in the annual report). If board members allow themselves huge amounts it will knock your dividends and stunt company growth. It's not unknown for directors to increase their salaries when profits have actually slipped some way. If this happens you might take it as a sign that those at the top may be more concerned with themselves than the real priority – your interests as a shareholder.

But it's quite a different cup of cocoa if the chief executive's pay is linked to the company's performance. This gives her a thumping stimulus to improve earnings which will soon show in benefits for the shareholder. As her whack increases so does your dividend and the value of your holding.

The higher management of companies also arrange share options for themselves. This seems like a perk which share-owners should object to. But it's not the case. For example, I have a modest slice of a smallish company which hit a bad patch and stayed on it. A new, well-regarded chairman was roped in at a comparatively modest salary. Is he mad, I thought? Why risk a good reputation by joining a small firm which you may not be able to save, for this sort of money? But then I noticed his vast holding of share options. Imagine that the shares are worth £1 each when he joins the board. He is given a lorry-load of options to buy the shares at £1.25 each. If he can turn around the company so that its shares rise to £1.50 he can sell his options, making 25p on each one. This is a heck of an incentive which should, of course, drive up the price of your shares.

Out of the Frying Pan?

Sometimes a famous manager will desert a large well-known business to join a minnow. Perhaps he yearns for a quieter life – and pigs can fly! Ambition is more likely the key. He hopes to expand his reputation and wallet by shoving a small, but promising, fish upwards until it becomes a high-earning whale.

This is normally done by sucking in other tiddlers along the way. If his acquisitions pay off, the share price will rise at speed. Of course, as Julius Caesar once said, ambition can stab you in the back. Many captains of small companies make the mistake of expanding too far, too fast. It can lead to destruction, and occasionally does. But if we're talking top managers, they shouldn't let it happen, and his appointment to a nondescript firm is normally welcome news for shareholders.

But how do you know if some respected executive is deserting a successful giant to become a big fish in a small pond? There should be some mention of the move in your newspaper. And if the article charts the transferring manager's past successes, all the better. Hopefully the move won't be treated as a major story, so most people will miss it. Otherwise the share price might rise before you can contact your broker.

Some companies swallow pride and go head-hunting for a fresh leader if profits begin to slide. They actively winkle out a new chief executive who has previously impressed the City by dragging up other firms by their bootstraps. Then they offer a high salary and share options to tempt him or her to jump ship. An appointment like this can put a cracker under the share price when it's announced, as professional investors have high expectations of new brooms.

The honeymoon is sometimes short-lived though. Despite new blood in the boardroom, the small firm may stay in the doldrums. This might be because the new boss's *modus operandi* doesn't happen to suit a company of modest size or perhaps because his luck has finally run out. As it happens, some professional investors never have faith in high-rollers in big companies who switch to smaller concerns. The worlds, they say, are too far apart. They'll only invest in a new chief if past victories have been won in companies of similar scale and functions to his new home.

And indeed, this story – enthusiastic expectations of a new highly-respected chief, followed by crushing disappointment – is common in the share world. Luckily, most City tales which seem to promise a predictable ending can be exploited by investors. The method here is to buy shares at the double on first hint of the new chief's appointment, and sell when the resulting rise halts and begins to slide. On the other hand, if you've heard good things about the new boss, and believe he's capable of pulling off a sparkling recovery, you could hang on to your shares until the results start coming through. But first check the company's latest balance sheet. Is there really a decent chance that the company can be turned around? Or is it odds on that the enterprise is so deeply in muck that not even a genius could save it?

How long do you give a new chief to save an ailing company before you jump ship? Well, don't expect immediate results. He will have an awful lot to do. Impatient investors can bail out too quickly, dragging down the share price with them. If you reckon the newly-strengthened board hasn't had time to turn things around, and the share price is falling too fast, you might consider buying some more stock at the reduced price. But when you do start to lose patience with the new broom, say goodbye.

Directors Who Buy

One of the more intriguing indicators of how well a company is doing is whether or not its managers are pumping their own money in. If some of the directors start buying extra shares, they are hardly likely to be expecting trouble. It's even possible that they've learned of some thumping good news which isn't yet public. So it's obvious, then. If we read that directors have increased their shareholdings, we should rush to the drawer for our cheque-book and follow their lead. But hold your horses!

A rush to grab more shares by directors isn't always what it seems. For example, there may be a take-over bid in the offing. Board members are unhappy about this and are fighting back. One way to strengthen their hand is to increase their personal stake. Then they'll have more shares under direct control, which is useful in case ordinary shareholders like us are happy to sell to the predator. We know that the share price of the target company often soars when a bid looks like succeeding, and slumps when it doesn't. Therefore, if directors buy huge parcels of shares to thwart that bid, then the share price is not going to rise at all, but slide back.

There are other ways in which a director's purchase doesn't necessarily signal a boom in the shares. The well-known television director David Mitchell is a modest investor on the stock market. He read that a head of a small public company had just bought more of the shares, though newspaper reports didn't specify how many. Impressed by this apparent show of confidence by an insider, David shelled out for £500 worth of stock. At the weekend he read a more detailed account of the director's transaction. To his chagrin he learned the director had bought far fewer shares than he had!

In this case, the director may well have bought a tiny amount of shares for the sole purpose of bolstering the resolve of both current and potential investors. And he's more likely to do this at a time when the company is entering choppy waters than when it's riding the crest of a wave. And there's another hidden motive for managers to buy extra securities in their own business. They hope the extra demand will push up the share price to placate their bank which may be getting jittery about growing debt.

But don't be down-hearted. Having given you a few reasons why director purchases aren't always a good omen, it should be said that most transactions of this sort do signify that the directors are super confident that their firm will prosper in the near or distant future.

Directors Who Sell

Now, what are we to make of the opposite situation: a director who announces that she has sold shares in her own venture? This sounds a bit ominous, doesn't it? Well, perhaps not. A sale may be necessary for all sorts of personal reasons. Perhaps the director has eyes set on a new mansion. Maybe the company has such glorious international expectations that she needs cash to buy a private plane. Or then again, perhaps she sees the writing on the wall for the firm and has started feeling for the ejector seat.

You should be a little more concerned about executive share sales if more than one director is involved. True they may all have personal reasons for the sell-off – but surely a group sale is more likely to be based on problems facing the company? And if every director on the board had sold shares, I think I would be really worried.

Ring 'Em Up

I've written down the names and phone numbers of all the big cheeses in companies in which I hold a stake. If things go wrong, I ring up to put them on the spot. They may not be ecstatic to receive my call, but only a daft executive would rebut an inquiry from someone whose money they rely on. I begin this little chat by making a polite request as to who is to blame for the set-back. This is more likely to rattle them than asking what went wrong. Then I offer a list of suggestions for improvement. It would be surprising if all of these hadn't already been considered. But you never know, one idea might have been overlooked. At least my call will let them know that one shareholder at least is ever so slightly hopping mad and expects better from now on.

But this isn't just a spleen-venting exercise. I listen carefully to the executives' replies, and if they are reasonable and contain feasible assurances for the future, I'm inclined to keep my money in. Whereas if I find myself fencing on the phone with a desperate nervous wreck, I might prefer to cut the cord. Or at least to take a top slice of any profits so far.

Some companies have only meagre contact with their private shareholders. If so, just one call might be enough to galvanise the board into a more effective battle plan to bump up earnings in future. As a broadcaster, I know that a single, but eloquent, letter of complaint from a viewer has often plunged television mandarins into deepest misery.

When speaking to a top executive, is she polite or rather off-hand with you? Do you have the impression that she regards you as a part-owner of the company (you are, you know) or as a bit of nuisance? If she's eager to help and not plainly anxious to get you off the phone, surmise this to be a good sign. The best directors work chiefly to increase their shareholders' returns. If a manager takes this duty seriously, it's probable your holding will increase its value. If she can't please her shareholders, the company will be starved of funds to expand, live long and prosper.

Pointing the Way

There are thousands of different forces, from obvious to esoteric to utterly unfathomable, which haunt the stock market. We need all the help we can get to make enough sense of it all to know when to buy, sell or leave the broker well alone. Ambitious share-pickers can't afford to neglect any pointers which might lead to success, even if they attract a certain amount of scorn. Here are one or two more controversial ideas from my contributors.

That Certain Feeling

Sometimes we really fancy a company's chances, but haven't a clue why. Yet the enterprise screams 'buy me' from the financial pages. Surely we should ignore this sort of hunch? There's no information to go on. Yet the itch won't go away.

Those new to share-picking might be inclined to close their minds to unsupported hunches. But investors with some years' experience often consider a small punt founded only on a gut feeling. Why? Because they know that thousands of scraps of City information are logged in our heads without us being conscious of the fact. This is possible because the subconcious recalls much more information than the aware part of the brain. Indeed, some boffins believe it remembers absolutely everything. The subconscious mind is capable of sifting through these hidden facts to form a conclusion which the conscious brain is only vaguely aware of. This could be why we sometimes get a compulsion to buy a share with seemingly little to go on. You might like to take advantage of this hidden 'computer' from time to time – by heeding its message.

Acting on a gut feeling is probably the most unsophisticated technique you'll ever use in the equity game, but many of the experienced share dabblers who've contributed to this book, say it shouldn't be ignored. (Though you should try to supplement such feeling with other more concrete reasons to make a trade.) Another, very annoying, aspect about inner feelings is the bitter regret we feel if we don't proceed on them and they prove to be spot on.

In the Mood

Some seasoned City observers believe that the stock market has moods. It may be in a good humour, in which case shares are buoyant, despite economic events to the contrary. Or it may be in a filthy mood, though the economy is in good shape. It all makes the job of predicting swings even harder. But the market moods aren't always arbitrary. They're usually reflections of the way the population happens to be feeling. This may explain why the autumn so often sees a bear run as people gloomily anticipate colder weather. And why the market frequently has an annual renaissance at Christmas. If the mood theory holds good you might expect the stock market to perk up if England was to win the World Cup and to slide horribly if a brewers' strike was to grip the nation.

Another human characteristic sometimes attributed to the stock market is its 'body language'. Very experienced exchange watchers claim you can tell if a market will rise or fall by simply looking at the pattern of prices across the board. When I asked for more details, nobody could really give me any. But there does seem to be a sixth sense at work borne of years of constantly gazing at the prices day in, day out.

Friendly Advice

A very few companies – they include some privatised ones – have shareholders in the millions. Others have hundreds of thousands of supporters. But some small firms have only a few thousand investors on the register. So if you hear good things about a minnow, don't be slow to pass the good news to your friends, relatives and colleagues and milkman – after you've finished buying its shares, of course. If your friend follows suit it won't make any difference to the price. But if he passes your tip to his cronies then, rather like pyramid selling, hundreds of punters may be put 'in the know'. You can never know if this chain reaction will happen, but it's worth a few phone calls.

Still on the subject of sharing ideas, an engaging idea is to build up a 'school' of friends, acquaintances and workmates who all do a bit of trading. When a member of the group picks up a good tip, the information can be rapidly circulated by phone. But you must all enter into a pact first. And that is: nobody should be blamed if the tip fails to perform. Ideally, the share should never be mentioned again – unless of course it proves a late developer.

Without such a safeguard, passing on 'good things' to friends can be hazardous. I remember giving a BBC editor six tips, all but one of which proved extremely remunerative. One share price quadrupled, two doubled. Only one share under-performed, losing a third of its value. Guess which one he reminds me of at every opportunity!

Beer Wigging

I know full-time investors who like to go to pubs and wine bars in or near the City. They come alone and prop up the woodwork. The main purpose isn't to drink, but to try to overhear the odd 'buy' or 'sell' tip. It's understandable. You do hear a lot of shop talk among brokers, traders and the like – in fact many of them are pretty well obsessed. And rather loud-mouthed, too. But would you really trust a second-hand share tip from somebody you didn't know? Well, if you're sensible you don't.

Still, there's a world of difference between rushing across to the pub phone, clutching your broker's number, and making a mental note of your overheard information so that you can do a bit of homework before you decide whether to trade. Hanging around pubs seems a bit on the extreme side. But you should keep your ears open whenever anybody rabbits on about their shares. If you hear a share-picker holding forth at a party, you could wander up and join in. But remember Bing Crosby's advice: if you're talking, you can't be listening. Carefully remember any hints, while remembering it's good manners to give some in return. Another helpful manoeuvre is to make friends with people in the share trading business whenever you can. Stockbrokers and financial journalists aren't always good company, but they ooze information.

Look Before You Leap

I was going to call this chapter 'Strategies to Avoid' until I realised I was offering myself as a hostage to fortune. The share world is so utterly unreliable, that my choice would no doubt become 'Strategies which have inexplicably started working against all odds'. Even so, here are some common investment tactics which my informants tell me to be wary of.

All Change? – Not Likely

You're fed up with your collection of shares. They don't seem to be going anywhere. You feel like cashing 'em all in to start again. Think twice before you do. Market experts advise against shaking out all your holdings at the same time. Sod's Law dictates that as soon as you do it, all your ex-shares will climb ever onwards and upwards to vanish among the clouds. If you decide to swap shares do it very gradually, company after company, just in case your reasons to change prove hopelessly wrong.

Silly Sentiment

When a share rises or falls more than it ought to on all the evidence, it's usually driven by what the trade calls 'sentiment' which doesn't have as cheerful a meaning in the money trade as it does normally. You'll hear some complicated definitions of sentiment from City professionals but it seems to boil down to being fashionable. It can apply to an individual company, as in 'sentiment is riding high in Lettuce Amalgamated' or to a whole sector of the market: 'sentiment has been poor in oil production lately'.

If sentiment is said to be strong in a company, it could be that lots of people rather fancy the share for no stronger reason than other punters do. Sentiment is often pretty powerful – for a time. If it's there, it can push up a share so impressively that others join the rush, shoving it even higher.

Less canny investors will buy shares when they've already become over-priced, hoping they'll continue to shine. But if there's nothing but sentiment to blow them up, the bubble will usually burst. As most investors have found, when there's a rush for the exit, not everybody gets out in time. My informants give two pieces of advice here. Don't buy dear shares in the dubious expectation they'll become even dearer. And avoid speculating on thin air. You should have at least one sound reason, and preferably lots more, before you trust a company to get it right. City elders will tell you: it's usually better to buck a trend than ride one.

Freebies

Some shares come bearing gifts. Their ownership entitles you to discounts on air travel, hotel rooms, insurance policies, clothes and so on. People, reading numerous press articles on the subject, are tempted to buy such shares for these 'bargains'. They are not always warned that dealing costs, the spread between buy and sell prices and stamp duties, often cancel out the discounts altogether.

Another drawback is that many companies stipulate that you hold a minimum number of shares before you get your perks – and this encourages you to hang on to a hefty holding when all the signs tell you to cull. If there's no limit on the amount of shares you can hold to claim the benefits, you can buy shares and then sell them all but one. Then you still qualify without risking your money. Though even this crafty dodge has dealing costs against it.

The reason I don't particularly care for share perks is down to blatant prejudice. Two companies which discount goods and services are in my portfolio and both are harbouring nasty losses. As a shareholder, I was also given a money-off card in a well-known chain which, very soon afterwards, troubled an administrator for his services. This is not to say that companies making offers to shareholders are less than sound – some of them are very profitable indeed. It's just that a few extra goodies shouldn't influence the choice to buy or sell shares.

Buying Foreign Stock

No hints specific to overseas money markets are included in this book. This isn't because investment abroad isn't worthwhile, because it often is. But each country needs a different approach, and shortage of space forbids it. And in a sense there's no need to invest abroad. British companies are becoming much more global. So many equities you buy on London's stock market are exposed to the ups and downs of foreign markets anyway. In fact, many large British groups have quotations on more than one stock market. Nearly all the major UK companies rake in huge chunks of income from abroad. For example, the average company in the FTSE index depends on the USA for a third of it's business. That's the main reason why Wall Street has such an effect on money markets here.

Unwanted Advice

Beware of people you don't know who try to sell you shares on the phone. These calls can come out of the blue, usually from firms based abroad. In fact dodgy share scams can hit you from all directions. I was once using an 'execution-only' broker who's not supposed to give advice. I'd just bought some shares in an aviation company, after reading favourable press reports. Before I hung up, the broker said, 'We've been recommending shares in a small leisure firm, sir, because we know the management and they're extremely good.' Being green and new to the game, with touching faith in brokers' opinions, I agreed to buy some stock. It was less than a year before I had grim news from a receiver, afterwards never to hear of the company again. Acting in a stupid fashion is a great teacher when it costs money. I have never since invested a penny in any company until I've investigated it enough to know that if it flops I can't hold my sheer ignorance to blame.

The Trading Trap

If brokers didn't charge commission, and there wasn't a difference between buying and selling prices (the spread) or an irksome stamp duty to pay, then we could all dip in and out of shares to our hearts' content. This would help us take advantage of very small up-and-down market movements, which are recurrently more predictable than big ones.

But as matters stand, trading is pricey enough to make over-trading a mug's game. I may seem like an AA man warning motorists about fog, but the only advice here is not to venture on to a phone until you're sure your trade is really necessary. Brokers, on the other hand, are quite happy with over-trading as it boosts their income. That's why their newsletters to clients contain bags of 'buy' or 'sell' tips, but very few exhortations to 'hold'. One trick to beware of is what the City calls 'the switch'. This is when your broker advises you to sell Brown's Crisps Ltd and buy The Black Sock Corporation in the same breath. They get two chunks of commission, you get a big invoice.

There are other ways to waste money by over-trading. You could buy too few shares in too many companies. Or you could sell shares in dribs and drabs, rather than all of them. Though it works out cheaper to trade lots of stock at the same time, some sellers get into a blue funk before parting with their shares, dreading that the price will shoot up the moment they put down the phone. So they dither at the last minute and sell some stock instead of all of it. They decide overnight that they should have sold the lot after all, disposing of the rest of the shares the day afterwards. They end up paying more because brokers make discounts for bulk selling. The moral is: if you're going to sell your stake in a company, you must have a good reason, so why not go the whole hog?

The consensus among investment professionals I've consulted for this book is that you should not buy or sell shares in blocks worth less than £2,000. Smaller trades are simply not cost effective. However, this advice is not quite as pertinent to cheaper shares. I, for one, don't relish trusting £2,000 or more to a penny share company. I have even bought £100 worth of shares on occasions, knowing that a 3p share can readily increase to 4p. If I can double my money, those who broker the deal are welcome to their costs.

Dividends

Though the thrust of this book is directed to making money from fluctuations in share values, there is lots to be said for the regular income which shares bestow if you keep them. It's to be remembered that a very large number of retired folk rely on share dividends for their living expenses. But if you can manage without this income and arrange for your dividends to be churned back into the company, the rewards are much higher. It's estimated that two thirds of the profit made by keeping blue-chip shares for a long time comes, not from the increasing value of the shares, but from ploughing back the twice-yearly dividends they produce.

Many people make the mistake of ignoring dividend income when they come to decide whether a share is worth keeping. Yet dividends which may seem pretty measly when the registrar's letter is opened at the breakfast table soon add up, specially if you've arranged to take them in new shares rather than cash.

One of the precautions you should always take before disposing of shares is to check their current yield first (oddly, that's the figure under the heading 'yield' on the financial pages). This figure can be seen as the equivalent of the interest you'd get from a building society though it may be higher. And look at the yield before you buy a share, too. If the yield is a low figure or non-existent, the company – if it's not a new venture which is still coping with its start-up costs – may be struggling. But if a company's yield is high, it doesn't necessarily mean the company is bobbing along nicely. To keep up appearances, dividends are sometimes paid from spare company cash – called reserves – even when there's been a loss. This keeps the shareholders sweet and stops them hauling their money out.

Timing is important if you are offered the choice of taking your dividend in shares or cash. Always leave the decision to the last minute. Should the share price take a drubbing just before the deadline when you must choose, the cash may be more valuable than the shares, so you should opt for that. But usually, shares given in lieu of a dividend are worth more than cash and should be accepted, if you don't need the readies. It is, after all, a chance to add to your holding without paying a broker's commission or the 'spread' between buying and selling prices.

Another reason to invest in a company which pays bulky dividends is that big institutions seem attracted to them. And, of course, a big investment from a big player is always good for the share price.

Is a Dividend Likely?

A board of directors has a choice whether to pay dividends or not. Sometimes, it all goes to clearing debt and buying buildings, machinery and stuff. If a company in your portfolio has not given you a share-out this year, and their reported profits don't seem too bad, write to the chief executive firmly asking for a dividend next time. The decision whether or not to pay a dividend is often hair-line, so your letter might just make a difference. And you could add to your argument by pointing out that if the firm pays regular dividends it encourages other investors to pump their money in.

Some types of company pay better dividends than others, because they've traditionally had room to generate lots of cash, even during recessions. They include medical companies (pharmaceuticals), electricity, water and gas suppliers (utilities) and banks and insurance companies (financials). Such firms can be past their peak when it comes to spectacular leaps in the share price, but their dividends are chunky – or jolly well should be.

But what if a company pays out a bigger dividend than the balance sheet really justifies? If you have a suspicious nature you might inquire how many shares are held by directors. If they've tucked away massive bundles of shares, they'll get a massive hand-out, but only if they announce a big dividend. Perhaps you don't mind, because you'll get a welcome cheque too. But there be drag-ons here. If too much money is drained away, the firm could suffer from lack of investment, and even go to the wall.

The investment manager of an insurance giant told me that one of his golden rules is to look very carefully at a firm which pays big dividends before risking his funds. If the profits don't vindicate the share-out, he stands aside.

Divining with Dividends

Numerous super-traders use dividends to test the health of a company – both present and future. If the annual and half-yearly pay-outs are chirpy, then the company is probably doing well now (with the reservations given above). But it may also flag that the directors have grounds to expect even better things in a year or two. It's an especially rosy sign if the dividend is maintained, or even increased, after a pretty disappointing year, as this almost certainly indicates that the firm expects a rattling good future. (Unless, of course, this is just a pathetic attempt to present a brave face to the City.)

Contrariwise, if company leaders fear that a falling demand for their products, higher running costs or mounting debt lurk around the corner, they will butcher the dividend, even after a recent run of unsurpassed profit. So if you spot that dividends are well down on previous years, be on your guard.

Crashes

A stock market crash comes out of a cloudless sky. (Though coach-loads of financial journalists will claim afterwards that they expected it all along.) Around 20 per cent is wiped off the value of major companies just like that. Perhaps more. Though stock market melt-downs don't threaten as much as doom-mongers would have us think, they are a worry. However, it's worth remembering that companies aren't damaged in a practical sense after a vertical drop in the markets. They still have all their assets and markets intact. And recovery has always been just a matter of time.

Can we predict a crash? Well, if equity prices have been rising for some time, there's a fair chance that some are defying gravity. Some fund managers cotton on to this in time and 'go liquid'. They sell their massive holdings to sit smugly on the cash. Word gets round the Square Mile. The herd instinct kicks in and others quickly follow. This is enough to light the blue touch paper. But crashes can also be set off by many other circumstances, including unexpected hikes in interest rates.

It took 25 years for Wall Street to fully get over the notorious Great Crash of 1929, but recovery after the 1987 world plunge took only two years. Nowadays, City professionals expect most market nose-dives to flatten out and rise to normal heights again reasonably quickly. The most optimistic of them say the spectre of crashes, as opposed to 'market corrections', is receding anyway for the simple reason that governments will do all they can to limit the damage.

Another bulwark against the possibility of crashes is a change of attitude by fund managers. They're no longer quite so anxious to swap stocks for cash when the markets take a turn for the worst. They now realise they can't win, even if they guess right and sell just before a collapse. Their problem is that pulling out of the market on a large scale confers a reputation for being over-careful, and in these fast-moving days, being labelled as a scaredy-cat is death for a fund manager. Super prudence doesn't endear you to your superiors or your investors who all exert pressure to make big profits fast. This may be a very unjust view to take of a poor chap who's only trying to stave off horrendous losses on your behalf, but it exists.

After the Crash

It's nice to have the foresight to sell shares before a crash. You can buy them all back afterwards at knock-down rates. But most experts advise you not to sell after the event. It's true, there'll be a few weeks of uncertainty when your shares may slide even more, but they nearly always come back.

The worst of a crash can be all done and dusted in one day. When Wall Street plunged 508 points, the index clawed back about a third of its value in the next day or two. This boomerang action is unfortunate in a way. There's not much time to take the best advantage of the drama. You are just thinking of which shares to buy at their new bargain level, when things get back to normal.

Actually, treating a sudden loss of market value as a buying opportunity *par excellence* can backfire on you. The panic may be difficult to abate and the market may fall even further. Should you buy straight after the plunge – or wait till the feathers settle? Most investment specialists I consulted on this point felt it's best to wait a few weeks, even months, till the market chooses its new level before buying anything. Few, if any, of my advisers thought that selling immediately after a crash was a good idea. I also happen to have a friend who got wholly dispirited and sold every share he had after the 1987 disaster. He put what was left into a building society – and now bitterly regrets it.

Crash Shares

Which shares should spark your interest after the crash? Obviously, you need to know how to spot a bargain. Have any well-known companies fared worse in the catastrophe than others in the same mould? If so, the market-makers may have over-reacted in their case. When other investors catch on, the price may resume its rightful place at the top of the market tree.

Or have you spotted a company whose shares have emerged unscathed? This could mean that fund managers think so highly of its cash-making potential that they're hanging on to the stock, even during a melt-down. We know that financial institutions spend an awful lot of money paying number-crunchers to identify companies with high earning power and delectable prospects. So if they do hang on to one particular batch of shares even when the market is disintegrating, then fund managers may be aware of all sorts of good things about the company which you aren't.

When it comes to pinning down a bargain after a crash, one investor I know is always one step ahead. He carries about his personal computer a hit-list of companies he fancies, just in case the market collapses. He won't buy them before a market shake-down when the price tags are high. But after a set-back, the shares can be expected to drop nicely within his price range. He can then snap up stock in luckless companies without wasting time on thought, because he's already researched them at leisure. Without his 'crash list', my friend fears he would get into a tizz and buy into some firms 'blind', pressured by knowledge that the market could spring back at any moment.

A Rights Carry On

When a company needs lots more cash it stages a 'rights issue'. It does this by offering existing shareholders cart loads of new equities. Just how many shares are held out to you depends on the size of your present holding. The offer is made on one new share for every two you already have, say, or one new share for every five you hold – or any other combination. These new shares don't come free – you are invited to pay for them by a certain date.

This doesn't seem much of a deal, does it? The number of shares in existence is set to explode so that company earnings will be spread more thinly. Yet you are expected to pour even more money into the company, when you never planned to.

Well, actually, most rights issues do benefit existing shareholders. This is because the new shares are usually at a brawny discount to what it would cost to buy them on the open market. Why? Because the company wants to make damn sure all their new shares are snapped up. Otherwise, their grand plans won't be worth a hill of beans. And worse, they may be landed with a crippling bill for organising the rights issue, all for nothing.

The discount on the share price on the Stock Exchange can be quite juicy. Offering them at half market price isn't unknown. There is a snag, though. When a rights issue is announced, the ordinary share price suffers – though not usually by much. It might even rise – if the City realises that your company is actually going to do something really useful with its new money. For example the firm might want to swallow up a highly-respected rival. If the view of this target is that it's a real snip, then the share price of the rights issuing company could mount.

My heart always lightens when the paperwork for a rights issue drops on the mat. For one thing, if I agree to buy the new shares, I won't have to pay a broker's commission. More importantly, the price of the new shares usually stays below the market price until I've time to sell them for a profit. Thirdly, it shows that the company I chucked good money at years ago has at last risen on its hind legs to actually do something.

To take up a rights offer, you must send your cash by a certain deadline. If you miss it they send your cheque back, which drives me up the wall. It can readily happen, though, as cunning investors always wait till the very last minute before taking up rights. This is because a sudden upset could make your entitlement of new shares dearer than those you could buy on the open market. Another reason not to send your money post haste is that they'll cash your cheque like a shot and you'll lose interest on your money.

But you don't have to buy the new shares. Supposing that as the deadline approaches the difference between the cost of the new shares and the old (known as the premium) begins to dwindle. Is it still worth jumping in? Probably not. If the cash your company hopes to raise by the rights issue is intended to launch a take-over bid, you might take a good hard look at the targeted company instead. Would your money be better spent buying shares in that firm? Could be. A handsome bid would send its equities into orbit. But before you put pen to cheque, see what the press has to say. There are bound to be opinions given on whether this particular rights issue is a peach or a lemon. It's also worth knowing that if you are strapped for cash to buy your rights, or if you simply lack faith in them, you can try selling them, just like shares, through a broker.

Advance Warning

Sadly, any money to be made from rights issues is usually limited to the lucky ones who already have a stake. Deadlines are set so that carpetbaggers can't hurriedly snap up some stock to take late advantage. But sometimes you do just have time. It is possible to read reports that a company plans to launch a rights issue 'later in the year'. You could then buy shares in this enterprise, hoping to be offered new shares at a big discount to the market when the time comes.

An engineering group, in which I had a small stake, came back on stream after trading was suspended for a while. The directors acknowledged that without extra cash they would soon be in trouble. They announced a rights issue would be held 'some time in the future' at 10p per new share. The shares were suspended at around 22p, but on the first day back in the market they traded around 15p. I decided to buy more stock at this price. I wasn't expecting the price to rise much and in fact it fell. I was more interested in the chance to have the right to buy the new shares at 10p each.

But this isn't an automatic way to turn a quick pound or two. You won't be the only one to read the news that a rights offer may materialise. Other punters will be thinking the same thing. The price may rise on the news, when by rights a poor performance should be nudging it down. By the time the rights issue is underway, the bubble may have burst, leaving you with a loss.

There's also a cynical view that directors could be tempted to make vague suggestions about a 'possible' rights issue without any real intention of going ahead. They would only seek to encourage more investors. However, the company would suffer severely from a loss of credibility when the event failed to materialise.

On the whole, top investors are enthusiastic for the money-making possibilities of rights issues. But there are always promising situations which turn into duds, so please look before you leap (as always).

Eggs and Baskets

One of the first nuggets of counsel we all pick up when we become share-pickers is not to haul your eggs around in one basket. In other words, don't buy all your shares in the same sector. If every equity you own is linked to oil, say, and there's a world slump in oil prices, your whole portfolio will suffer.

I once broke the rule by investing in three different supermarkets at the same time – Sainsbury's, Tesco and Asda. There were rumblings that all three companies were abandoning their latest price war. I thought the news would beef up share prices all round. But the battles must have taken their toll. Shortly after buying into all three companies, Sainsbury's gave a profits warning and its share price was pole-axed by nearly a third. Tesco and Asda fell in sympathy, of course, and I was left nursing a sickening loss. If I'd only had one retail food share in my basket, instead of three, I wouldn't have all the egg from that one basket on my face.

How Many Eggs?

As well as choosing different sectors of the market in which to buy your shares, really prudent investors scatter their funds over a large number of companies. If you rely on just four enterprises and one collapses, then it's serious. If you have 20 share certificates with different names at the top, big losses posted by two or three companies won't send you looking for an outside ledge on a tall building. Some brokers urge their clients to buy an interest in just 10 businesses. They argue that this is a nice manageable group and that it's hard to keep track of any more.

If, however, you lack the skill and energy to grind away at gruelling research, you may end up investing in several dogs, so it may be safer to put your faith into more than 10 companies. Personally, I keep a thumb in 50 to 60 pies at any one time. This is abnormal – the action of a share addict who likes to boost the chances of something happening to his portfolio every day. Actually, having shares in so many companies isn't as expensive as it sounds. I have only risked a few hundred pounds in some of the more chancy firms.

Running a heavy portfolio doesn't mean you can sit back and

forget all about your investments on the dubious grounds that there are too many firms to monitor properly, and that you're protected by sheer numbers from any gallumphing losses. You should still keep an eye on daily prices and read as many financial pages as your time allows. In fact, having loads of companies to follow makes press research more interesting, with probably at least one of your 'babies' in the news every day.

There are investment gurus who disapprove of sowing money over too wide a field. They say it's like betting on most of the horses in one race. Yes, you're more likely to win, but your bets on losers dilute the winnings. Of course, you can afford to back more nags if your selections are running at long odds. In investment terms, this would mean having lots of penny shares in your portfolio. The rewards can be greater, but so are the chances of coming unstuck. So unbalancing your portfolio with too many penny shares doesn't seem like a good idea.

By way of a trivial aside, may I mention another benefit of keeping a hefty number of companies in your portfolio? It gives you the opportunity to attract a devil-may-care reputation by casually mentioning your losses, when, looked at in its entirety, your share collection is actually making a healthy profit. Alternatively, you can do what some share tipsters do and crow about your successes, while drawing a veil over the failures which outnumber them.

The Spice of Life

There's another way to spread your risk other than choosing companies in different lines of business. You could pick enterprises in similar sectors, but which vary in the way their future prospects are likely to be achieved. In other words, you place in your portfolio companies which are all set to take different routes to success. These might be blue chips with a steady upward gait, small 'growth companies' likely to get bigger, concerns crying out to be taken over, penny share firms with new stronger management and so on. Choosing companies with such varied characteristics will help give you a nicely-balanced portfolio. One which is top heavy with the same kinds of company is somewhat risky.

Basket Critics

The tactics above are ways of spreading risk by not putting all your eggs in one basket. But many investment gurus say you will never amount to much as an investor if you diversify too much. One of them was legendary economist John Maynard Keynes, who died in 1946. He wrote: 'To carry one's eggs in a great number of baskets without having the time or opportunity to discover how many have holes in the bottom, is the surest way of increasing risk and loss.'

He also argued: 'As time goes on I get more convinced that the right method is to put fairly large sums into enterprises one thinks one knows something about, and in the management of which one thoroughly believes. It's a mistake to think one limits risk by spreading too much between enterprises about which one knows little, and has no reason for special confidence.'

Put in a different way, the Keynes system was to investigate a few firms thoroughly and put your trust in them, and no others. To stuff your portfolio with lots of companies, he felt, was to take too many shots in the dark.

But just because Keynes was a great economist, was he any great shakes as an investor? Well, not at first, he wasn't. His speculations in the markets began in 1919 and left him penniless by 1920. He was only saved from bankruptcy by a friend. But he changed his strategies in the thirties to include his unfashionable views on egg baskets. And then all changed – his trading fund of less than £10,000 had grown to half a million pounds in five years. Of course he made use of other systems as well, some of which appear in simple form in this book.

Those investors who tend to make the most money in the markets agree with Keynes that buying into too many companies secures lacklustre profits. Gains from the winners will be neutralised by the losers. Spreading your investments over a wide area is also criticised by analysts who constantly try to identify the next sector of the markets to outperform all the others. If you find the 'magic' sector, they argue, then you should certainly invest in more than one firm belonging to it.

Even if you invest in two companies in the same sector, you can still protect yourself by diversifying. How is that possible? Well, you could invest in two companies which do the same thing, but operate or make their sales in different countries. An obvious example is in the field of oil production. You could invest in a company whose source of supply is the Far East and in another which pumps it out in the Wild West.

Tools of the Job

There are plenty of City folk who do well out of shares without actually investing in them. They write about them, recommend them, broker them, or buy them with our money. The legion of City professionals do very nicely out of these activities, without any of the danger. But do we risk-takers do nicely out of them? Read on. . .

Using the Press

If you don't work in the City, your sources of information are far fewer than those who do. You have little more to go on than company reports and media coverage. As we've seen, the stuff in company reports can be hard to fathom, vulnerable to 'creative accounting' and out of date. This leaves press reports (and much sketchier coverage on TV and radio). But even a lazy investor like me should study the financial pages – not just detailed reports in posh papers, but snippets in the popular tabloids and local rags, too.

  Reading the papers brought me two of my finest hours in the share world, hugely increasing the value of my portfolio and giving me confidence to turn share-picking into a part-time career. Both

148

windfalls followed favourable press comment on the companies concerned. They were only short scraps, but my guardian angel was on duty and they caught my eye.

The first piece was about a television company which had lost its franchise causing the shares to sink eventually to 4p each. Totalled up, the entire share value of TVS wasn't worth the site it stood on. But TVS had a card up its sleeve – a bumper library of programmes, including some classic comedies from America. The newspaper commentator simply said the shares had to be worth more than 7p which was their stock market showing at the time. I could see the logic of this, but by the time I'd decided to buy the shares, they'd plunged to 4p each. I bought £500 worth. Soon afterwards TVS aroused the interest of an American TV company. The shares began a daily ascent and I bagged some more when they reached 9p. The shares rose quickly to about 40p and I sold out near the top, making almost 1000 per cent profit in a few thrilling weeks. I bought a Volvo estate car with the profits. This bonanza for lucky TVS shareholders is still talked about today.

My second stroke of luck, courtesy of a press article, came when British Aerospace hit a bad patch. Orders were drying up and the shares dipped to £1.50 each. A national newspaper reviewed the firm's present position which didn't seem too good. However, the writer added that the country couldn't afford to lose a company which made such a significant contribution to its defence. She expected the government to step in to save British Aerospace if its fortunes slipped any further. I invested £1000 and, when they rose to £1.90 each within a few weeks, I nibbled the cherry again. As I write British Aerospace shares are over £14 each. But though I did extremely well out of British Aerospace, I didn't stay around till the peak, because I have decided, rightly or wrongly, that I'm not really comfortable with companies linked to military aircraft.

Looking back, the British Aerospace investment was made for a pretty negative reason. I now realise that, I bought stock because I didn't think the share would drop much further, not that it would rise to its former eminence. City grandees would be proud of me for acting on that old chestnut – avoiding losses is the real key to success.

I wish I could say the two cases above are typical sequels to tips I've read in the papers. But I've also made losses by following the commendations of journalists. Just like analysts, brokers, fund managers and everybody else in the City, columnists get it wrong as often as right. You have to decide if the writer tells a convincing story or not. I happened to think the hypothesis about the government stepping in to rescue a struggling British Aerospace rang true. I also agreed with the hack who thought it unthinkable that a firm with the strong assets of TVS wasn't attractive to somebody out there. Sometimes though, under pressure from a City editor, a correspondent will hype up a story on slim facts, especially if she claims a scoop, and you must be prepared to read between the lines. Read each press article very carefully, and listen for alarm bells, before you buy or sell on the strength of it.

Brokers

You can pay hefty commissions to a broker who will give you buy-and-sell advice as well as placing your order. Or you can choose an 'execution-only' set-up which is cheaper. Which service you choose depends on your knowledge, your confidence and how thrifty you are. All I will say is that some brokers' advice is useful, some isn't and some is worse than awful.

If you do opt for an advisory broking firm, try to ask for the same employee when you phone. You should also make an appointment to meet her in the flesh when you can surreptitiously test her knowledge.

This book isn't one of those investment manuals which explain the mechanics of share dealing, so I won't bore you with the protocol of making a trade. But when you place your order it is worth chatting up your broker. This won't get you too far with an 'execution-only' merchant (as Sir Walter Raleigh once said) but you can pump an advisory broker for useful City gossip. I'm extremely civil, if not oily, with brokers on the grounds that they'd be less than human if they didn't have favourites. I'm hoping they'll save their best tips for my ears only. They'll almost certainly be happier to stay on the phone chatting to me (a really nice bloke) than to the grumpy old colonel one always imagines to be the archetypal stockbroker's client.

However experienced you are, use your broker as a sounding board for your ideas. If she sneers at your views on a share, don't buy it anyway out of spite. Ask for details. You might like to ring off while you consider her opinion before making a trade. After all, she's closer to City gossip than you will ever be.

Some brokers send you a monthly bulletin with 'buy', 'sell' and 'hold' tips. Study these closely. The firm would be unwise to allow a sloppy analyst to send out dubious tips to clients – they'd soon lose business. Having said that, I once read carefully the weekly tips of an analyst working for a broker. I sold when he said 'buy' and bought when he told clients to 'sell'. It was only a perverse experiment, but I still made a little money.

Newsletters from brokers sometimes use heavy jargon in a misguided attempt to impress. It wastes a lot of time translating it. My current broker, who is very good, sends me faxes three times a week. I'm not sure the extra day's saving on the post is of great market advantage, but when seemingly red hot tips are wired in under their noses, it sure impresses friends!

Unit Trusts

A popular way of spreading risk through many companies is to buy unit trusts. Sounds a good idea and many careful people will only invest in the stock market in this way. After all, the selections are drawn from the research of analysts who really know their stuff. In reality though, some trusts make a loss, and really good returns are rare. This is because fund managers tend to follow the pack. Also, unit trusts levy big commissions.

If you believe the advertisements for unit trusts, you'll expect some scintillating returns. But the administrators pick their dates carefully. Most adverts appear only when the Stock Exchange is enjoying a cracking good run. You're meant to be impressed by the figures on display and buy some units. During a market recession, few unit trust adverts appear. But, as we've seen, buying in a buoyant phase is often the worst time. The recommended period to buy any share product, and that includes unit trusts, is when the markets are at a low ebb. The financial groups who manage unit trusts often run many different ones. This allows them to pick out the best performer in their pack, trumpet that it's done fantastically well and casually disregard the mediocre showing of the rest.

Another drawback is that there's very little fun in unit trusts. They don't rise and fall as quickly as shares, and the exciting decisions are left to the managers. Private investors have nothing to do – other than to choose when to pull out or stay in.

Tip Sheets

These are weekly or monthly newsletters which give several share tips per issue. You buy them through subscription. As an ex-subscriber, I've made big money from their suggestions – and lost almost exactly the same amount on others. Tip sheets have a tendency to produce advertising literature which makes a big fuss of their fruitful hints, while ignoring their dogs. Their editors claim a lot of research is done before recommendations are made, and that's probably true. But you may feel you get enough advice from your newspaper, especially as the cost of most tip sheets is on the high side. However, if you like to invest in small firms, tip sheets which specialise in this area can be worth it, as the press gives most space to leading companies.

When your tip sheet arrives in the post, you may think there's an advantage in calling your broker within minutes, before thousands of fellow readers nip in. It's not the wisest course, though. Market-makers also read the sheets and they may tinker with the price of shares featured in them even before the rush begins. The share may reach new heights for a few days, but once the excitement abates, the share's price may snap back to square one. Unless the tip sheet's analysts predict an imminent take-over bid for a company you're interested in, it's unlikely to do much harm if you wait for a month or so before committing yourself.

Season Reasons

We have already looked at the times of the day, and certain points of the week, when it may be best to buy or sell shares. But beyond those daily theories, it's also been found that certain months of the year can be linked to bull or bear markets. Some months attract buyers, some seem to put them off.

Summer Blues

August is often a dismal month on the Stock Exchange. Many private investors prefer to spend their cash on basking under foreign suns than stumping up for equities. This could interfere with the share values of small companies. More significantly, fund managers also leave the City in droves at this time of year. For those with families, the August school holiday is the only convenient time to take their leave.

A parallel situation applies to public auctions. Many auctioneers refuse to hold important sales in high summer because too few buyers attend. If a sale does go ahead, competition for lots is scant, because there are too few buyers in the room. So prices fall. Astute

154

antique dealers know this and attend auctions in August because there are plenty of bargains to be had. The same rationale applies to the stock market, making August a good time to procure shares and a poor one to sell.

The summer weakness in share prices often, but not always, spreads into September and October. It's tempting to think that share buyers, spent-up after their summer holidays, are compelled to sell rather than buy. But share-pickers don't usually live from hand to mouth (or shouldn't do) and anyway it's the captains of unit trusts, insurance giants and pension funds who really steer the market. Perhaps the real reason is that we all find summer inertia hard to defeat.

There are always modifications to trends in the stock market, and August isn't always a flat or falling month. If June and July have been below par, there is sometimes a small rally in August. These late summer buying bursts are short-lived and soon wither as autumn draws on. But if shares don't fall, or at least stagnate, in late July and August, it often means the September market will fall even further than normal.

Awful Autumn

While leaves were falling in 1987, so were share prices on Wall Street. One unfortunate American lost £308,000,000. The shock wave was immediately felt over here, though it took two days for the news to sink in. On what became known as Black Monday, the British stock market lost an eighth of its value. By next day, nearly a quarter of all share values were wiped out. It was October 20th.

An earlier autumn also saw another whopping financial catastrophe – in fact the worst of them all. The hideous Wall Street crash of 1929 took place on October 29th. The autumn effect has a long history. Back in 1720, lords, ladies and fat cat merchants were investing in the South Sea Company set up by the British government to open up trade in goods from South America. To try and wipe out national debt, it offered stock to the public. They weren't exactly penny shares, either. Share prices rose from £128 each to £1,050 in a few months. Eight weeks later, the South Sea Bubble popped and share prices spiralled down to 175p each – and were still falling. Date of the bursting – September 23rd.

There was another shock in early autumn 137 years later, at the end of a burst of enthusiasm for the newfangled railways. The market collapsed when eagerness to buy stocks suddenly evaporated. And in September 1873, Austrian and German land prices dived causing local banks to give up the ghost. There was a world-wide slump and Wall Street closed for 10 days.

What causes so many disasters to take place in the autumn? Could it be mass depression brought on by the end of summer and the spectre of winter? Has the fear of autumn among investors, caused by the Wall Street Crash and Black Monday, become a self-fulfilling prophecy? Is there a mysterious cycle at work, perhaps even started by the South Sea Company debacle? Is it those sun spots again? Nobody really knows. But it remains true that an awful lot of City professionals are now pretty wary about buying heavily from mid-September to the third week in November.

Christmas Markets

Early in November, private investors often sell more shares than usual. Is this because, when the cash comes through in two weeks' time, it will be timed exactly right for the annual Christmas shopping spree? If so, it makes the week around Bonfire Night a satisfactory time to seek out bargain shares, especially among smaller companies which are propelled by individual punters.

But, I hear you say, only people on a tight budget would need to realise assets just for Yuletide shopping. Surely, anybody so short of readies doesn't trade in shares much anyway. *Au contraire*, people with the share bug often commit all their funds to the cause. They leave hardly a sou (I seem to be turning French) in a low interest bank or building society account. And I know some investors who always cash in some shares for Christmas expenses. They know it's silly to put all their money into shares, but they do.

In the last few days before Christmas, shares often begin selling again. This could be because the stress of preparing for Christmas starts to be outweighed by high festive spirits. Hope reigns. Everything will come good in the New Year, including the share market. Some buyers (nincompoops all) may even be a little tiddly when they ring their broker. They could buy shares worth £3,000 in an enterprise in which they would only risk £300 if sober.

Christmas Tips

Another possibility why a rush develops before Santa comes to town is that share addicts risk withdrawal symptoms if they don't delve in the market before the holiday break. Only by dealing at the last minute can they shorten the tedious holiday period when the Stock Exchange closes down. By the same token, you'd expect there to be a similar dash to trade shares as soon as the markets re-open after Christmas. But as the big fund keepers take as long to shrug off a party hangover as the rest of us, the immediate post-Yule market is a boring place where prices are usually fairly static.

Putting the more whimsical reasons aside, the major reason for the frequent clamour to buy in the last few shopping days before Christmas is more practical. As we miserably traipse around shopping centres, looking for last-minute ideas, we jostle battalions of other souls doing the same thing. There always seem to be more shoppers than last year and we imagine this signifies a bumper Christmas in the stores. Because we anticipate some astounding December sales figures to be announced in January, we dive onto the phone to snaffle shares in chain stores now.

But Christmas sales figures are just as likely to disappoint as they are to cheer the City. Sometimes spending booms, sometimes it doesn't. It's reliably unpredictable. Share specialists have told me it's a mistake to take the size of crowds in stores as a yardstick. Customers may be doing less shopping this year, but all at the same time. They could be buying cheaper presents. Instead, the experts advise a bit of telly watching. It's a set piece for store managers to be interviewed on pre-Xmas news bulletins about their seasonal takings. If the manager of Boots says buying is strong, then it's a much more reliable pointer than your Aunt Dot remarking: 'Boots was pretty empty yesterday, love.'

Spring Fever

After the post-Christmas blues, the urge to buy can return to the markets in January, only to be followed in most years by a late winter gloom in February. This deflated patch may be seen as a handy buying chance as share prices should soon recover, and begin to act like sap in early spring – by rising. Then you may care to obey traditional City wisdom which urges investors to 'sell in May and go away'. This translates as: take the summer off and don't consider investing again until the market booms again in December.

As with all other market indicators, none of these seasonal changes is guaranteed. They may all happen in one year. Or just one of them will apply. Or even none. But it has been noticed that if the market does veer from the traditional season pattern to any large extent, it can mean a very nasty plunge is on its way.

A Sunny Day in London Town

Some rather obvious scientific studies have left no doubt that the weather affects our moods. If it's sunny, we're bright, breezy and optimistic. On grey days, as you'd expect, we're dull, apathetic and pessimistic. I've looked in vain for any experiments to prove that climatic changes influence dealings on the Stock Exchange. But most market experts I've talked to think they do.

If the theory holds, then blue skies should improve the market, as a surge of mass cheeriness leads to extra buying. While falling rain means falling shares. To stand a chance of profiting from this idea, then you should buck the trend and do the opposite: sell in the sun and buy in a downpour. But, you ask, if there's something in all this, why do prices often degenerate in the summer and surge at the year's end? Well, as we've said, lots of big players desert the Square Mile to go abroad in the school holidays – and anyway you know what British summers are like.

Earnest chaps in white coats will never be able to measure the effects of sunshine on the money markets because too many other mysterious forces pull and push. But it may be safe to say that if share prices are going to take a dive, perhaps the falls won't be as steep on balmy days as in freezing, murky fog. I know it seems far-fetched to link the weather and share prices. But the idea doesn't seem so improbable if you acknowledge that we all feel more optimistic when the sun shines. I for one sometimes wait for a sunny day before I dispose of a holding, unless there are pressing reasons to sell under cloud. But as I won't go under a ladder on the way to buy my *Financial Times*, perhaps that's just me being superstitious.

April Showers

A deluge of shares is sold towards the end of March and beginning of April. Tax accounting has a lot to do with it. You get an annual capital gains tax allowance of a few thousand pounds which is set every year. If you haven't turned enough of your profit-making shares into cash in the 12 months before the April 5th deadline, you can't claim the whole allowance (it can't be carried over until next year). So investors are frequently panicked into selling huge bundles of shares just before April 5th, to take full advantage of this tax break.

Lots of shares which have shed value during the year are also traded in just before the April deadline. This is so the sellers can establish a loss which they can use to cancel out any taxable gains made during the year. With all this selling going on, the early April stock market is likely to be depressed. So this is a good time to buy. Those who want to sell, other than for the tax reasons, should come to market another day.

If the stock market doesn't fall far at the beginning of April, then it could be buttressed by another lever working in the opposite direction. This is the time of year when some punters make a last-minute dash to acquire a personal equity plan (a PEP). We're only allowed one PEP a year and the right to buy one can't be rolled over. So the rush to pump money into equities inside a PEP can be urgent. (PEPs are a share-picker's dream. You are allowed £6,000 worth of shares in a group of companies and another £3,000 in a single enterprise, all free of tax on dividends and capital gains. The most satisfactory PEP for share-fans is the self-select type where you make the choices.)

Another April effect on the stock market can be brought on by the weather. A cold spring gives an unexpected boost to oil, gas, coal and electricity shares. Heavy use of heating fuels is inevitable in winter, of course, but that's already built into prices. An icy April is an extra bonus for companies which provide heating fuel and power, as the extra sales won't have been taken into account. A chilly April extends the winter heating period by around 13 per cent. So when an icy spring threatens, don't cast a clout till May – and don't cast off any shares in a company which supplies heating.

The Taxi Driver Theory

A few City observers support this seductive theory, but I've named it after the cabbie who first drew it to my attention. It's heavily based on mass psychology – and it says that a large part of the human race inclines towards doing the same thing, all at the same time. Sounds fanciful, but let's look at the facts. It's agreed that carloads of us take off to the coast on a fine bank holiday Monday. This is an instance of many people sharing a common idea at the same time. Another example is that most of us go to a polling station on election day. But the taxi driver theory goes one further. It proposes that we all suddenly decide to do the same thing on a certain day, not because it is a special day, like a bank holiday or polling day, but because it's a day which comes at a fixed period of time after that special day.

One particular day when we all feel like behaving in the same way, according to my cabbie, is the fourth Saturday after Christmas. How on earth does he work that one out? Well, most of us have a hectic time before Christmas when we try to cram in shopping between office and family parties and many other exhausting functions. We become worn out, and few of us feel like going out for quite some time. This feeling takes about four weeks to wear off –

and then we are all raring to go out again. This is where my cabbie comes in.

He's noticed that on the fourth Saturday after Christmas his trade picks up in the evenings, while during the day many more shoppers than usual fill the streets. The following Saturdays are comparatively quiet until, another four weeks later, everybody wants to be out and about again. He believes these waves of activity follow a few weeks after all sorts of 'special times' including bank holidays, Bonfire Night, Easter, school holidays and so on. Of course, the waves don't apply to everybody, but the theory says that enough people do behave in the same way to make such mass motivation a possibility. It may sound fanciful, but academics who've measured stock market movements believe fervently in waves and cycles. They don't always know what sets them off. At least my cabbie has identified some starting point for his 'mass activity cycle', like Christmas and bank holidays. The theory seems possible if not entirely plausible. It would explain why town centres are almost empty some days and teeming with bodies on others. If these activity cycles occur then perhaps they affect money markets. Maybe we can work out which weeks are more likely to attract buyers and which periods will see most selling. This would help to guess what the 'crowd' is apt to do at any one time, then do the opposite. It's just a thought.

Keep Your Eyes Peeled

A few shopping days before Christmas, my brother saw something normally only associated with East European countries: a long tail of shoppers outside a high street store. There was no 'Winter Sale' advertised and the doors had been open some hours. Here was a pile of stock, he thought, everybody needs to have. He decided to buy into the action.

But with the usual Yuletide chores pressing, he never got round to ringing a broker. And, of course you've guessed, the shares doubled within the year. He still didn't fork out, believing it to be too late, and the shares climbed another pound each. In fact, this store did so well, there was talk of handing back some profits to shareholders.

Ever since this family tragedy, I've stalked the aisles of all stores listed on the Stock Exchange. Some have been almost uninhabited, others teeming with folk. Needless to say, I haven't bought shares in any stores which I found to be sparsely populated. But not all those shops which I found to be stuffed with people have wooed my money, either.

Many top investors also creep about stores. And they've told me to watch the tills, not count the crowds. Some shops, not just those selling books, attract more browsers than buyers. Yet it's cash taken and credit cards swiped which count – not the number of gawkers coming through the doors. To help discover if a store is really doing

163

well, don't just note the length of queues at cash desks. Also take into account the quantity of tills and number of cashiers serving. And listen. If you can hear electronic cash registers tootling away, there's a splendid chance that those annual results just a few months away, will set share values soaring. Don't just snoop on cashiers on Saturdays or lunch-times, though. Business should be brisk on Tuesday mornings and Thursday afternoons too.

Super Snoopers

Some of the biggest names in the Footsie are supermarkets. They are ever anxious to go one better than the competition. As an investor, you need to know which one is likely to win this battle and so attract more customers. Fortunately, they make it easy for us. Supermarkets often operate side by side in not-so-peaceful co-existence on the same out-of-town site. You may prefer one chain to another, but as an individual you don't matter if the crowd has different tastes. Check which store is fuller and which car park has the poshest vehicles in it. Make your checks over several days of the week just to be sure and then, if you feel like investing in a food retailer, you have an easy indication of which way to go.

But you have to be careful with supermarkets. They keep building more of them. Yet the population is fairly static and we're supposed to be getting more health conscious. So are we all going to eat more food to boost earnings by these extra stores? I doubt it. Some investors I know wouldn't touch a supermarket share with a disinfected barge-pole because they can't see they have any room to grow.

Pint Punting

Sadly, in the course of research, you must force yourself to visit a few public houses. The Stock Exchange is stiff with pub chains. If you find a hostelry bristling with affluent folk, all drinking and eating and keeping a large bar staff on its toes, it's likely in these homogeneous days that every other establishment in the group is also coining it in. If the shares have been flying high recently, you may be too late. But if the financial pages show they've been languishing for a time, you might give it a whirl.

Fancy a pizza share? If you can find a pizza emporium which is always full, preferably with loads of greedy children, it might be worth a try. But never invest in any kind of restaurant, unless you've dined there first. Are prices low; are the staff friendly, enthusiastic and happy in their work? Do they taste all right (the pizzas, I mean)? If not, stand aside.

Toy Story

Shares in toy companies are a favourite among investors. They know that parents (except themselves, naturally) nurse a compulsion to cave in when pressed by a squeaky voice for the latest and

most expensive toys. Even during the worst recession, there will always be a mum, dad or more likely besotted grandparent to spend a last tenner on something junior absolutely must have.

You know which toys are a hit with your own children. Does the manufacturing company make lots of other things the kids really like? If so, consider procuring the shares. But if they rise sharply soon afterwards, it's sometimes best to realise your profits, as trends and fashions in the toy world can vanish as fast as car keys down a drain.

Weather Bother

The weather can be a friend or foe to share followers. Wind is one of the enemies if you have stock in an insurance company. Prolonged gales cause widespread damage which eats into profits. The odd blow won't make much difference, but if storms start affecting a large chunk of the country, it may be worth looking up a long-range forecast to see if they're set to continue. If they are, sell your shares – particularly if the firm in question specialises in building insurance, rather than motor vehicles.

Droughts also knock insurance companies. They shrink the ground holding up houses and the subsidence claims which follow are heavy. Even if your own area is not affected, other parts, particularly London which is built on untrustworthy clay, may be having a terrible time. So keep reading the newspapers.

It's not just our weather which erodes insurance profits. Many British companies insure foreign customers, especially in the USA. This is why you should keep up with news of hurricanes and big snow falls across the Atlantic.

Home Truths

The state of the housing market is a reliable guide for share dabblers. It would be surprising if shares in building firms didn't power ahead during a buying boom. And when interest wanes – possibly provoked by accelerating interest rates – it's time to sell. You could also consider the many other businesses which benefit from the fortunes of building groups. Take estate agents for instance. Their shares are extremely vulnerable if nobody is buying bricks and mortar. But their profits rise very steeply in a housing boom.

Do-it-yourself stores suffer terribly when everybody stops moving home. But once houses start shifting again, new owners dash to change the decor. Suddenly, paint, tiles, flooring, plastic ponds et al, start selling like hot cakes in a snow storm. Yet the boost in sales at DIY stores usually takes some time to come through to affect share prices. So as soon as house prices start to move, coupled perhaps with a helpful drop in interest rates, you might want to do a bit of spending on DIY shares. A bit further into a housing boom, shares in garden tool makers, garden centres and seed suppliers also start to gain ground.

Germ of an Idea

Every so often Britain has a flu epidemic. Occasionally there's an even bigger outbreak, known as a pandemic, which strikes whole continents. When this happens there's naturally a rush to the doctor's to be vaccinated. There are only a few pharmaceuticals companies making a flu serum so when the illness strikes on this sort of scale, they turn some nice profits. Yet some winters manage to escape the worst ravages of flu and only routine vaccinations take place among the elderly and patients with chest complaints.

There's little point in buying shares in a firm making flu vaccine if you have no idea if a major outbreak is round the corner. However, the World Health Organisation meets every summer to decide if a pandemic is likely to happen. Rather like share chartists, they attempt to read the future by looking at the pattern of past outbreaks. The Department of Health will order more vaccine if they give warning of a pandemic, so share prices might rise, even if flu doesn't decimate the country. If a pandemic warning is given by the World Health experts, you will read about it in the papers.

Just the Job

Newspapers and money magazines aren't the only places where you can pick up useful facts to help your share trading. Somewhere to keep your ears pinned back is your place of work. My line as a consumer journalist is extremely useful as I hear criticism and praise of dozens of companies every week. If there are really lousy firms about, I'm often the first to hear about it. But nearly all careers give opportunities to pick up juicy information on shares to buy, sell or run a mile from.

Bus drivers will know whether their firm gives better service than its rivals. Computer programmers are aware which high-tech firms get it right. And garage mechanics know who makes the strongest, most reliable, cheapest car parts. If you don't work in any of these jobs yourself, you could always quiz somebody who does. But be careful if a friend raves too much about his own company – he might only be boasting.

Do any firms which you deal with in the course of your work seem to have cornered a market? Are they so indispensable that it's becoming impossible to deal with anybody else? Are they raking it in? Then they may be worth a small investment.

You may also be able to buy equities in your own firm, if you're happy with its progress. But not every employee can do this. If you have access to the company's accounts for instance you'll be barred because of insider trading rules. Be sure to let your boss know if you have bought a stake, by the way – he'll never think of sacking a shareholder!

Tune In

All kinds of TV and radio programmes carry information which bears on shares. An antiques show could tell you that valuations are booming after years of stagnation. Those higher prices will bring in more profits for auction houses quoted on the Stock Exchange. A radio series about books will advise you which publishers are doing well.

TV programmes for motor enthusiasts give clues, too. If their test drivers rave about a new family car, thousands of viewers will be impressed. They will tell their friends. Garage firms will order more of this certain model. But should the programme criticise a new car, sales will slow, causing shares in the manufacturer to take a back seat.

I know one investor who strained his eyes to try to spot what particular make of computer was being used behind BBC news readers. He figured that if the news-room used one brand of computer, then every other department of the corporation probably had it too. And before placing such a strapping order, it was only fair to licence-payers that a lot of shopping around had been done to check quality and price. My friend argued that if the TV company was impressed, after all its research, then it followed a lot more firms would also be impressed and buy the computer, too. My friend ordered a bundle of shares in the computer company and was glad he did.

Hot Tips

The weather has a dramatic effect on the path of some shares. In a drought, companies you should be wary of investing in include:

- water companies
- plastic pipe makers (your flowers may need them, but hose-pipe bans hurt business)
- foreign holiday promoters (sun-seekers will stay here)
- makers of rain-coats and umbrellas.

But you might be interested in companies who make:

- watering cans, garden furniture
- sun cream
- swim wear, cycles, sailing dinghies or sports equipment
- ice cream or soft drinks.

Obviously, you should reverse this advice during a chilly, water-logged summer.

As you'd expect, beer, lager and cider sales are all up in a long spell of hot weather. But not necessarily if they are sold in pubs. It's the take-home trade which really reaps the benefit of long-lasting tropical sunshine. Firms which specialise in stocking off-licenses and supermarkets always do better than pub chains and their suppliers.

Wintry weather also has a bearing on share prices. Gas, electricity and fuel oil is in more demand so shares rise as temperatures plummet. If you have a feeling in your water that a long freeze threatens to set in, you know which shares to buy. However, once a cold snap is underway, the value of fuel shares will have already risen. The trick is to try to predict its coming. For those who believe in less scientific methods, you might bear in mind that severe weather in the USA is usually reckoned to arrive here about three weeks later.

Old Ideas

As the population grows older, all kinds of businesses will benefit. An easy example is the expansion of homes for the elderly. Quite a few groups quoted on the Stock Exchange have an interest in these. Drugs companies and suppliers of medical equipment also face a healthy future. And builders making sheltered homes, coach tour operators, stair lift engineers, opticians and walking-stick makers should flourish, too.

Boots

Perhaps you wouldn't imagine car boot sellers and the gentle souls who run charity shops to be a big threat to the City. But together these amateurs make a formidable selling force. And none of their profits find a way back into companies to benefit shareholders. Look at the facts. My very small town has four charity shops. They're all busier than every other shop in the market square. It's happening all over Britain. Gone are the days when the only customers of second-hand goods were hard up. Some people buy all their needs from charity shops – except food and medicines.

The other threat to normal commercial selling in Britain is the car boot sale. They're becoming bigger and more popular by the

minute. Clothes, hardware, toys, office gear, garden stuff, are there in abundance, but everything is sold. Toys and children's wear are particularly well traded. You have to approve of car boot selling (and charity shops) because it's a recycling exercise on a grand scale. But their activities are a warning to the City generally and to chain stores most of all. Economists have noticed that people have become much more reluctant to pay increasing high street prices. It could be that the humble car boot sale with its low, low prices have contributed to this resistance. On the good side, a refusal to pay too much curbs inflation, but it also impedes earnings. It makes you wonder if investors should beware of putting too much faith in the future of chain stores. It may be true that some customers can't bear to buy anything which isn't new, but their numbers are diminishing and so is the stigma of buying second-hand.

Are You Being Served?

Your car has a prang. You need it for work. You have a young family. You live in an isolated village. You are stranded until the car is back on the road. Yet the insurance company won't sanction repairs until their inspector has seen the damage. The days pass by and he still doesn't come. Is this an insurance company which finds it hard to pay out on claims? Your natural inclination is never to buy shares in this company. Well, perhaps you should think again. At least you know that if your case is anything to go by, the company have no tendency to throw money away. If they are reluctant to pay out to all policy holders it may lead to bigger earnings for shareholders' profits. On the other hand perhaps word is getting round that they're slow payers and disgruntled customers are turning to other insurers in droves.

As an investigative reporter, I have probed dubious goings-on involving supermarkets, chain stores, insurance companies and banks. I always checked the share prices of these companies in the *Financial Times* next day. I expected, arrogantly perhaps, that my programme would cause so much disquiet among listeners that they would dispose of their shares in revulsion. Yet usually the share values actually rose. Coincidence? Or is it (as we investigative journalists say)? Or did a lot of new investors hear my report and learn to their delight that profits come before customers for this particular company?

This cynical view is probably fanciful. But I will add this: whenever I exposed a crooked lawyer, accountant or architect on the radio, I had phone calls to the office asking for the delinquent's telephone number as they happened to need the services of a crooked lawyer, accountant or architect, unquestionably for some dark deed or other.

Faulty Goods

A good reason to stick your head in boiling tar rather than buy equities in a company is if you have been failed by one of its products. If your new TV is fuzzy, if your toaster pops up while the bread

stays where it is, if your baby's disposable nappy leaks after a heavy drinking session, you ought to draw the line on investing in the manufacturers. If the products suffer from poor design, thousands of customers will share your dissatisfaction, and they may have to be withdrawn. Share prices will pitch over backwards. But even if none of this happens, imposing your own boycott on the company's shares is a minor way of getting your own back.

All Change

Some nice people invest in a company because they once owned one of its products and 'it lasted 20 years with now't ever going wrong, no not once'. But this isn't a sound reason to leave your shares to fester, in spite of more promising opportunities elsewhere. Anything could have happened. The firm may have been taken over and the old directors long gone. Manufacture could have been switched to a country with lower standards. There may be nothing left of a familiar product but a familiar brand name.

Brands Snatch

Next time you see a group of school children in the street notice their clothes, shoes and bags. Their gear will nearly all have the same maker's logo on it. This manufacturer is so trendy that kids feel they must buy its stuff – and nothing else will do. Or rather their parents must.

You are seeing the exalted power of the brand name in action. Firms with strong exciting brands attract eager customers. Because their logos are not just popular, but nearly compulsory, they can command higher prices than their rivals. This is one heck of a competition-beater and it makes investors feel safe.

Another advantage of a famous brand is that the firm behind it can launch other quite different and untried products with the same trademark. Customers buy these unfamiliar things from the outset. Because they're familiar with a much-loved logo on the packaging, they instantly associate what's inside with splendid value. This is why some of the all-time great investors will only buy into companies with a powerful, ubiquitous brand.

By the way, before you ring a broker to buy into a company with a beefy brand, first find out the name of the company behind the brand – it may not be the same.

To Keep You Sane

As I said at the beginning, share-picking should be a jolly affair – not a grim obsession. But, of course, it can get on top of you – especially if your portfolio is having its own bear run. Let's look at a few ways to keep a positive outlook – whatever happens.

Comforting Thoughts

One of the commonest gems of advice dispensed by City observers who contributed ideas to this book is not to sit on your losses too long in the hope they'll go away. Yet, there are times when lots of signals suggest that the market has got it wrong and your share may indeed buck up if you keep it just a bit longer. Here are some encouraging thoughts to fortify your beleaguered spirits as you hang on.

- When a cod shows signs of injury, it becomes more attractive to a shark. Similarly, as its share price hurtles downwards, a company seems a better bargain for anybody contemplating a bid.
- Few things concentrate the minds of directors and get them off their bottoms more than a falling share price. The value of their personal holdings and the chance to cash in share options come under fierce attack.
- When an enterprise hits choppy water it may organise a rights issue to raise extra cash. The new shares will be offered to existing holders at a discount. This saving could be quite hefty, as it's otherwise hard to persuade shareholders to pump more money into a sinking ship. When you sell these new shares you may even be able to cover your loss.
- When you eventually sell disappointing shares, you can use the loss to reduce the capital gains tax on your winners.

Don't Look Back

It's a harder decision to sell a holding than it is to buy one. We kid ourselves that every loser will bounce back. For that reason, once you sell all your shares in a company you should delete the transaction from your memory. For good. Remember Lot's wife. When she glanced over her shoulder at an overcooked Gomorrah she changed into salt. You may also turn white if you look back to check the progress of the share you sold. There must be no peeping at the price afterwards to see how it's doing. It could be dangerous to do so. If you look back and see an improvement in the share price, you may inflict a self-injury with your boot. You might also be tempted to buy the shares back in again.

It would be too easy to forget those sensible, well-thought-out deductions which led you to sell in the first place. Even if the price does leap afterwards, the chances are that those same reasons still apply and the enhancement won't last. So once you've sold your holding, forget it. Can you remember that?

If Onlys

This advice, related to that given above, refers to a kind of self-torture which is very common in the share game. There are many troubled folk out there who spend their lives regretting 'sell' decisions they've made. Sometimes these transactions were made years ago, but they still think about them at least once a week. This bitterness is powered by their ex-shares' starring role on the Stock Exchange ever since. It's an awful thing when the share you sold for £1 a year ago is now valued at £10 and seems unstoppable week after week. It's rather like dropping a dull boyfriend who later develops into a Prime Minister.

You have to train yourself to be philosophical about such disappointments. Like Julie Andrews, you should think of your favourite things – shares still in your portfolio which have scaled even greater heights than the ones you chucked out. If you hadn't sold when you did, would you have released the funds to buy into those other big winners?

Oh, Oh Portfolio

All your shares in different companies bear the same name – the portfolio. It's one thing and should be regarded as such. It either yields a profit or it doesn't.

So don't say Apex Biscuits made me £1,000 or Blackberry Toys cost me £500. Rather say: my portfolio has earned (or lost) £3,000 this year. This is the healthy way to assess your progress. A lot of gloating about successes while forgetting the turkeys is common among investors. It's a hazardous self-deception because it leads to wild speculations instead of thoughtful investing.

To stop you believing you are doing better than you are, balance up your profits and losses at least every month. It won't take long, especially if you have a personal computer. You may find that your talent as a share-picker is limited and you'd be better off with a building society.

Inquests

A share slides away making a whacking dent in your portfolio. You dispose of it. Never mind, the loss isn't quite as damaging if you can salvage some valuable lessons from the set-back by holding a post mortem. Sit down by the fireside and contemplate what went wrong. Were you too hasty in buying? Did you have at least two good reasons to wade in? Did you investigate the management and the market prospects? Was the share performing better than the average for its sector? If you can identify just one mistake you made, then it could save lots of money in the future. It's worth thinking very hard to isolate a hidden error. It could be your Achilles' heel. You might be making the same gaffe over and over again without realising it.

The Twelve Top Tips

When I was collecting all my 'rules of thumb' for making money in shares, a few tips popped up more than others. On the arguable theory that the favourites should be the best, I repeat them here. Commonly stated though these hints are, some are without universal approval and others probably appeal to more cautious investors. There are also 13 suggestions not 12 – but then the best books always give the reader a little extra.

- Spread your money between many different sectors
- Look for slow but steady risers which rarely falter
- Wait for a good success story to meet up with a bargain share price
- Never buy on a rumour
- Buy into a company if its rivals are doing badly
- Follow leading companies
- Buy firms with a low share price compared to rivals in the same sector
- When there are conflicting signals, get out
- Don't be too eager to sell when there's a panic on
- When hesitating over whether or not to sell a share, ask yourself if you would buy it now. If not – sell
- Good management is the key

- Don't take profits too early if the share keeps rising
- Don't be greedy.

The last point is the hint of hints as far as the contributors were concerned. If one of your shares has performed nicely, but seems to have run out of steam, don't hang about in the hope of it adding a few more pence. Get out before the spell breaks and wholesale profit-taking sets in.

Epilogue

Poker players like to tell you that they play a game of skill. So it is, but luck plays its part. If you draw four aces you'll probably win. But if you hold a poor hand, any amount of expertise and hard work won't save you. Luck and ill-fortune stalk the share world, too. That's probably why a fund manager of a big institution does well for years, then hits a ropy patch. When the tide turns, all the hard analytical work, talent and experience of her team still can't help. If things start to go wrong for you, do what I did, and pull out of the market for a year. Do a lot of reading before you come back to it.

Yet you should never regard investment in shares as a science which can be mastered. The serious work of analysts is impressive and is taken very seriously in the City, but it is largely based on events of the past. There's not much evidence that what happens then will repeat itself in the future. Though I hope all the hints in this book will help tip the balance in your favour, it must be emphasised that there are no certainties or guarantees in the share game.

So please, please don't invest more than you can comfortably afford as that would be . . . share folly.